IN HIS FOOTSTEPS

In His Footsteps

*The Priest and the
Catholic Charismatic Renewal*

by
Richard J. Pettey

PAULIST PRESS
New York/Ramsey/Toronto

IMPRIMATUR
✤ William E. Cousins, D.D.
Archbishop of Milwaukee

August 10, 1976

Library of Congress
Catalog Card Number: 76-45274

ISBN: 0-8091-2007-0

Published by Paulist Press
Editorial Office: 1865 Broadway, N.Y., N.Y. 10023
Business Office: 545 Island Road, Ramsey, N.J. 07446

Printed and bound in the
United States of America

Contents

Introduction

At the turn of the century small charismatic groups began to emerge on the North American continent, often revivalist bands of evangelizers from the Baptist tradition. But to the astonishment of many, in the mid-1960's these charismatic groups began to appear in several of the Protestant churches and, incredible as it seemed, in the Roman Catholic Church. Since the mid-1960's these groups have continued to grow in all the churches. The growth in Catholic circles has been such that there are a number of Catholic charismatic groups today in every diocese in the U.S.A.

The growing presence of Catholic charismatic groups means that these groups and Catholic priests will be encountering each other with growing frequency. Yet because of the newness of charismatic renewal, many priests are uninformed and apprehensive about these encounters. They find themselves asking: Who are these people? Where do they come from? What is this "charismatic renewal"? Do I have anything to offer them? Can I guide them? Or should I avoid them?

This work is an attempt to answer these questions. It begins in Chapter 1 with some historical background and a general description of Catholic charismatic renewal. Chapter 2 offers a brief sketch of the role of a priest in the Catholic Church as is found in the Vatican II document *Decree on the Ministry and Life of Priests*. Chapter 3 presents a new application of Vatican II's theology of ministry to the charismatic renewal, resulting in a rather practical explanation of the pastoral role of the priest in the Catholic charismatic renewal. This work is intended not only to give priests a job description for working with charismatic groups, but also to give the people of God in charismatic renewal groups a clearer conception of what they can expect of their priests.

1
Catholic Charismatic Renewal

I

1. Before 1900

Charismatic renewal is an ancient and continuing activity in the Church of Jesus. Ever since the beginnings of the Church's life, the people of the Church have been endowed with Spirit-ual or charismatic gifts, gifts yielding spiritual results far beyond anyone's natural expectations. These charismatic elements have continually renewed the people of God. The Church began with Pentecost, an indeed remarkable charismatic event, and has in every age since been the mother of charismatic renewal. This renewal has been personified many times in the paths of history. Iranaeus (c. 200), Tertullian (c. 210), Venerable Bede (c. 730), Hildegard of Bingen (c. 1200), Dominic (c. 1220), Anthony of Padua (c. 1230), Vincent Ferrer (c. 1420), Francis Xavier (c. 1550), John of the Cross (c. 1590), Teresa of Avila (c. 1580), and endless more like them were charismatic persons with charismatic gifts, the human instruments that God used for renewing his Church.[1]

3

The path of renewal is not a smooth path. There has always been a tension in the Church between the institutional and the charismatic, the Spirit acting from within the formal structures and the Spirit acting from amid the general Christian people of God. The two balance each other. It is not good for the Church to be over-structured, bureaucratic, legalistic, and authoritarian. But neither is it good for it to be free-wheeling, anarchistic, uncontrolled, and prey to whims and fads. The history of the Church shows a constant interplay between charismatic development and institutional stabilization, the one always checking the over-eagerness of the other. Charismatic renewals in the Church have raised cautious reactions from both theologians and authority figures, as Louis Bouyer is quick to point out. The former emphasize the need to discern the spirits and insist that charismatic phenomena not be pursued for themselves, while the latter are anxious to avoid eccentric and sectarian movements, yet remaining persuaded of the need to never quench the Holy Spirit.[2]

One should not think, however, that renewal is the sole property of the Catholic Church. Many of the non-Catholic Christian churches have originated in the spirit of renewal, often in reaction to the Church's sometimes oppressive institutionalism. Before entering a discussion of the modern elements of Catholic charismatic renewal, then, in the interest of historical perspective, it would be wise to briefly survey some of these non-Catholic approaches to charismatic renewal. One such early non-Catholic reform movement grew from John Wesley's fiery and reformist preaching (c. 1750). He was indeed charismatic, so much so that in the hindsight of history he is often called the father of the Pentecostal Movement.[3]

The nineteenth century was peppered with renewal and revivals in both the old and the new world, with nearly every movement being a renewal of the people's experience of God. Some movements were ecstatic (the Shakers), some were quiet (the Quakers), but all sought an experience they did not seem to be able to find in the institutional churches, whether Protestant or Catholic.[4] There was a new church formed even in Scotland-England in the early 1800's called the Catholic Apostolic Church, which in a prophetic way was a sign of the about-to-come twentieth-century Pentecostals.

The Catholic Apostolic Church appears to have had no direct influence upon the present-day charismatic or neo-Pentecostal movement. Yet its history, its teachings, its theological stance, its concerns bear striking resemblances to the charismatic movement.[5]

But it wasn't until the beginning of the twentieth century that the real revival began in the United States, or anywhere in the world for that matter. The famous Azusa Street and Topeka meetings took place at the turn of the century, sprouting churches which have never stopped growing.

2. Classical Pentecostals

It was 1906. William J. Seymour, a black Methodist minister, was leading his little Los Angeles congregation on 312 Azusa Street. The surprise was overwhelming when he and his people began to experience what they called a special anointing in the Holy Spirit. They prayed in tongues and prophesied. The little house soon filled with people and rocked with the Spirit that had ignited them.

Strange as it seems these same events happened in another place, too. It is sometimes debated whether it occurred before or after Azusa Street, but it did happen that a similar experience took place in Topeka, Kansas at a certain Charles Parham's Bible School. Parham and his people experienced this same baptism in the Holy Spirit and spoke in tongues. And then came Chicago. In 1908 W. H. Durham brought word of this new experience from Los Angeles to Chicago, and soon Chicago began to manifest the same phenomena as Azusa Street and Topeka. People were praising God everywhere. A new revival had begun,[6] and it spread like wildfire. All over the nation there were revival meetings, itinerant preachers swarming the continent and spreading this Pentecostal experience to the farthest parts of the continent, even to other continents. The effects of this movement remaining to this day are astonishing:

Pentecostals can point with justice to the worldwide sweep of their movement within half of a century. . . . Pentecostals can already claim, for example, that they are the largest non-Roman Catholic communion in France, Italy, and Portugal in Latin Europe, and in Brasil, Chile, and El Salvador, and perhaps also in Mexico in Latin America.[7]

The sects which have flourished in the wake of this revival are, among others, the Assemblies of God, the Holiness Churches, the Pentecostal Churches, and the Jesus Only and Latter Rain movements.

The progress of the Pentecostals, however, has not been without its pitfalls. They have had some difficulty in their development. Most notably, they suffer from doctrinal disunity. They are plagued with as many doctrinal variations as they have churches. The prime example is the teaching concerning baptism. Right from the beginning there was discord. Parham and Seymour recognized a three-stage way to salvation: *conversion*, also called regeneration and often symbolized in water-baptism; *sanctification*, the further purification of the heart necessary for the Spirit to enter; and *baptism of the Spirit* with speaking in tongues, the complete influx of the Holy Spirit. W. H. Durham, however, did not recognize the second stage, claiming that it is rather a process which continues throughout life. His doctrine, then, was a two-stage way: *conversion* and *baptism of the Spirit* with speaking in tongues.[8] Both of these two schools of thought are common in today's various Pentecostal sects, not to mention other variations of the same doctrine that have sprung up.

Despite their doctrinal disunity, there are many elements of Pentecostal doctrine that can be described in such a way that they are generally (but always with exceptions) acceptable to the Catholic Church. Some examples would be their doctrines that Jesus is the Lord, that the Holy Spirit blesses believers generously with spiritual gifts, that God is the Father, that Jesus redeemed us by his death and resurrection, etc. Yet in other ways the Pentecostals deviate from Catholic doctrine. Pentecostal doctrine always begins with the Bible. But for most Pentecostals, the Bible is the result of a direct, verbal inspiration from the Holy Spirit. It is thus the infallible word of God, always without contradiction and never contrary to reason. The Pentecostals are strongly fundamentalist in their interpretation of the Bible. Modern scriptural interpretation is looked on as demonic. Such theories as evolution are regarded as the certain roads to atheism or agnosticism.[9] It is in this ground of the literal interpretation of the Bible that the entire Pentecostal doctrinal system is rooted.[10]

Central to Pentecostal doctrine is that experience from which the movement has derived its name, the experience of the Holy Spirit as on Pentecost, called baptism of (in, with, by) the Holy Spirit. The Pentecostals accuse mainline churches of being "stuck between Easter and Pentecost."[11] The baptism of the Spirit marks the in-flowing of the Spirit into an individual and is always accompanied by speaking in tongues, which is the one sure evidence that the baptism has taken place. (This differs substantially from the Catholic approach to tongues.) It begins a fundamental and radical change in lifestyle, wherein one becomes joyful and learns to live according to the urgings of the Spirit. This experience is distinct from conversion, which is a previous step leading up to the baptism of the Spirit.[12] The passages of Scripture most commonly cited as the basis of this doctrine are Acts 2:1-4, 2:38, 8:4-25, 9:1-19, 10—11, and 19:1-7.[13]

Along with the baptism of the Spirit there come spiritual gifts given by the Holy Spirit. One gift which the Pentecostals say the Spirit always gives is that of speaking or praying in tongues. It is a vocal, and "non-verbal" as they say, prayer form, sometimes in a language not known to the speaker but known to others, and in other instances in no known language. It is sometimes ecstatic but is more frequently "cool," that is, the speaker is in complete control. Prophecy, another gift, is different from speaking in tongues. It is a message in the vernacular intended not for God but for the listener. It sometimes reveals the future, but more often is a word of encouragement or admonishment spoken in the name of the Lord. The gift of interpretation is the ability to understand the basic content of the speaking in tongues, and thus to tell the group in the vernacular what was said in tongues. Sometimes an interpretation is a prayer of thanks and praise, other times a prophecy. Another gift is that of healing, whereby a person is blessed with the power of God to heal both physical and spiritual illnesses. Gifts such as these the Spirit bestows as he wills. They may come at any time after the baptism of the Spirit. There are many more gifts, far too many to be treated in this work.[14]

The spiritual gifts are exercised most often in the context of the prayer meeting. The Pentecostal prayer meeting is lively. People participate in song and pray with vigor and enthusiasm. They are full of joy and express it openly. Sometimes the prayer borders on ecstasy, bringing an explosive quality to the group. The ministers are those who are given the particular pastoral gift of leading prayer. They conduct meetings which are often long but rarely drawn-out.[15]

Pentecostal ethics is rigoristic. Pentecostals usually tithe, keep a strict Sunday rest, will not participate in military activities, and have strict regulations concerning food, pleasure, and sex, including numerous taboos of dress and make-up for women.[16]

Four further areas of Pentecostal doctrine worthy of mention but beyond the scope of this work are eschatology,[17] ecclesiology,[18] demonology,[19] and sacraments.[20]

3. Neo-Pentecostals

Only fifty years after the rise of classical Pentecostalism, the Pentecostal experience began to seep into some of the mainline churches. The same religious phenomena that were experienced by Pentecostals became the experience of Lutherans, Presbyterians, Methodists, Congregationalists, Episcopalians, and others.[21]

Probably the most well-known organization for promoting the Neo-Pentecostal experience is the Full Gospel Business Men's Fellowship International (FGBMFI), founded in 1953 in Los Angeles. It has been successful in spreading the Pentecostal movement in Protestant circles. Their monthly publication "FGBMF Voice" witnesses and documents many of their experiences in the Spirit.[22]

One difficulty that the Neo-Pentecostals are experiencing, which is probably at the root of the mixed reactions officially and unofficially expressed by the upper structures of the churches involved, is the problem of bringing along "cultural baggage" from the classical Pentecostal churches.

There is a classical Pentecostal subculture or contraculture, which includes speech patterns, prayer postures, mental processes, expectations. This culture belongs to a specific historical, socio-cultural context, where it has its own validity. . . . Neo-Pentecostals very frequently forget that cultural baggage which has validity in one cultural context does not have validity in another. Cultural baggage is not transferable.[23]

It seems, though, that Neo-Pentecostals are beginning to learn that this baggage is not transferable. One small but important sign of this is their tendency to call themselves "charismatic" instead of "Pentecostal." This tendency is also common in the Catholic charismatic renewal.

4. Catholic Charismatics

"The Duquesne weekend" has come to be recognized as an hour blessed for charismatic renewal in the Catholic Church. In February 1967 a group of about thirty students and faculty members of Duquesne University in Pittsburgh spent a weekend in prayer and study, considering especially Acts 1—4. Nearly all who came had heard of the Pentecostal experience, and one or two had actually experienced being baptized in the Spirit through a local Neo-Pentecostal group, but none had any intention of steering the weekend in this direction. However, as the weekend progressed, each member of the group was led spontaneously to a deep experience of the Holy Spirit, not unlike being baptized in the Spirit.

There was no urging, there was no direction as
to what had to be done. The individuals simply
encountered the person of the Holy Spirit as
others had several weeks before. Some praised
God in new languages, others quietly wept for
joy, others prayed and sang. They prayed from
ten in the evening until five in the morning. Not
everyone was touched immediately, but
throughout the evening God dealt with each person there in a wonderful way.[24]

Some of the immediate results of the weekend
were these:

In the ensuing weeks the Lord touched many
others through this group; some turned from
lives of sin; others from intellectual doubt
turned and embraced the Lord Jesus in mature
acts of faith.[25]

Ralph Keifer, one of the people at the Duquesne
weekend, brought news of his charismatic experience
to his friends on the Notre Dame faculty. After experiencing the Duquesne weekend, he phoned Notre
Dame to relate what had happened. A small group
of people at Notre Dame gathered to pray about the
matter, and they too were baptized in the Holy
Spirit. This group eventually formed into a regularly
meeting prayer community, which grew and bore
fruits similar to those of the Duquesne group.[26]

A similar weekend occurred at Michigan State
University in April 1967. Forty-five persons from
Michigan, assisted by people from Notre Dame,
"were powerfully touched by the Spirit that after-

noon, and a deep sense of joy and love was communicated to the entire group, melting into a unity."[27] This was accompanied by numerous experiences of charismatic gifts.

Weekends and prayer sessions such as these began to occur across the country, some as direct offshoots of the Notre Dame and Michigan experiences, and others, amazing to say, quite independently of either. Included among the former is the Benedictine Abbey of Benet Lake, Wisconsin, whose roots grew from the Notre Dame community in 1969, and whose influence was to reach Milwaukee by 1970.[28]

Estimates of the number of Catholics involved in the charismatic renewal by 1970 range from 10,000 to 20,000.[29] Estimates of today's involvement are substantially larger:

> The charismatic renewal is the fastest growing movement in the Catholic Church today. There were few participants when the movement began in 1967, but by 1975 an estimated 500,000 Roman Catholics were involved on a regular basis. This rapid growth shows no signs of tapering off.[30]

This last estimate is not limited to the United States, but includes persons from many continents.[31]

II
DESCRIPTION OF THE CATHOLIC CHARISMATIC RENEWAL

This section will consider some of the theological-doctrinal matters concerning charismatic renewal within the Catholic Church. It is not correct to presume, even though many of the Catholic experiences are parallel to those in classical Pentecostal circles, that the Catholic theological description of these experiences is the same as classical or Neo-Pentecostal doctrine for they are different in many instances. It is clear, however, that while classical doctrine is in a theological culture that often differs from Catholic doctrine, there is no doctrinal conflict between the Catholic charismatic experience and the doctrines of the Catholic Church. This is rightly so, for if both are from God, then both are true and thus non-contradictory. There is only one true doctrine. One should be hesitant, though, to be judgmental about classical Pentecostals who have never had the advantage of having a firm doctrinal system or even the time to develop one. There are many ways to express the truth in human language, and theirs is their own best attempt.

1. Baptized in the Holy Spirit

The expression "baptized in the Spirit" is indeed unfortunate. It is theologically misleading. While it is the verbal symbol for a real religious experience, it is far from being a perfect symbol because it conjures up images that have little to do with the experience. It is the same expression used by classical Pentecostals, but in Catholic circles it has a decidedly different meaning. It is difficult to keep the classical connotations out of the Catholic meaning. Knowing that there is only one baptism and yet calling this further experience a "baptism" leads to confusion. Is it baptism in a broad sense or baptism in a narrow sense? Or is there even a difference? Is being baptized in the Spirit a new sacrament? Doesn't a person receive the Holy Spirit when first baptized into the Church? It would seem that an expression like "renewal in the Spirit" would be wiser than "baptism in the Spirit" because, as will become clearer below, the experience of being baptized in the Spirit is not a new influx of the Spirit, who has always been fully present in every baptized Christian. It is rather a renewal of one's baptism by the Spirit who was given at baptism much in the character of the Easter vigil's baptismal renewal rite.[32] Much misunderstanding by Catholics could be overcome if this or a similar expression were used. However, because there has not yet been a common effort to use such a new expression, the expression "baptism in the Spirit" will be used throughout this work.

The New Testament witness does not refer to a *baptism* of the Spirit but to *being baptized* in the Spirit. James D. G. Dunn, a theologian at the University of Nottingham, has devoted an entire book to a discussion of the New Testament witness concerning this being baptized, and in his conclusion he takes exception to the classical stance of having two baptisms, claiming instead that in the New Testament being baptized in water and in the Holy

Spirit are one and the same event. Thus there is no justification for saying they are temporally or spiritually separate events. He goes even farther and says that the New Testament witness forces one to conclude that anyone who has not received the Spirit is not yet a Christian.[33] Dunn has perhaps unwittingly defended a most Catholic position! Catholics would disagree with him, though, when he says that water is a mere occasion for the reception of the Spirit and not an instrumental part of the rite.[34]

Even though the New Testament witness concerning baptism is somewhat fragmentary, there are some well-grounded conclusions to be drawn. One of these conclusions, drawn by Donatien Mollat, is that the New Testament teaching on baptism includes the element of personal experience on the part of the baptized, experience in this context meaning "an order of knowledge, the immediate knowledge of concrete reality."[35] The baptized immediately knows the Lord and his Spirit, experiences his sonship. "The experience of the Spirit is the realization of the new being that Christians have become in Christ Jesus."[36] Especially (but not only) in John one sees experience in a place of primary emphasis. "John's thought insists more upon the experience of the Spirit as knowledge of the truth, incarnate in Jesus Christ the Son of God, the living revelation of love."[37]

In each Christian baptism the baptized person receives the Holy Spirit, but that is not the end of the sacrament; it is merely the beginning. Schillebeeckx recalls that the revival of a sacrament is not foreign to Catholic theology.[38] In fact, this is precisely the point of baptism in the Spirit. It is a revival or renewal of the sacraments of baptism and confirmation that have already been received. More specifically, it is the personal appropriation of what one has already received in the Church. It is a sacred moment when persons commit themselves and dispose their spirits to fully receive what was first given to them in the sacraments of initiation.[39] Hence the experience of being baptized in the Spirit is often a time for deep renewal, even immediate reform, and a soul-stirring event. For others, though, it is a milder experience, sometimes undetectable at first, which shows its fruits only after a time.[40] There are ample witnesses for both kinds of experience. Baptism in the Spirit is unique for each individual, just as God's love is unique for everyone. He can only love a person as that person. His gift of the baptism in the Spirit is tailored to one's own growth. Everyone needs renewal on occasion; fortunately the Lord understands human faltering. He provides special gifts of renewal designed to help each person grow.

That which is called being baptized in the Spirit is "an interior work of grace that only God can perform."[41] This is all too evident from the fruits which it bears:

While no two people will have the same experience of God, the most common fruits of being "baptized in the Holy Spirit" are increased attraction to and joy in prayer and the reading of Scripture, a deep sense of peace and the presence of God, an awareness of God's purpose for one's life, and an inclination to join with others in the praise of God. Frequently, Catholics are drawn to the Eucharist with a devotion they had never known before. Often, "being baptized in the Holy Spirit" prepares people to mend broken or damaged relationships. Some recommit their lives to Jesus Christ after a long estrangement; some experience healing in a disintegrating marriage.

This experience of the presence of the Holy Spirit is not merely something on the level of human emotions. It is something that affects the whole person, intellect and will as well as body and emotions. It is God as a person touching us as persons, revealing himself to us, calling us to himself.

Quite often the experience of being baptized with the Holy Spirit marks the reception of one or more of the charismatic gifts. This is not to say that a person was not gifted to serve the Church in the past. But additional gifts are commonly given, frequently the gift of praying in tongues.[42]

The reception of spiritual gifts, especially praying in tongues, while a common experience at being baptized in the Spirit, is hardly necessary. The Holy Spirit is not limited by human desires in his manner of renewing.

It is wise to note before proceeding that while classical Pentecostals claim that there are two separate baptismal experiences—conversion (water baptism, the work of humankind) and baptism in the Holy Spirit (the work of God), Catholic theology is quite the opposite, claiming only one baptism, of water and the fullness of the Spirit. Baptism in the Spirit is for Catholics not a sacrament, but the renewal of the sacramental Spirit.[43]

The experience called baptism in the Spirit is firmly placed in the writings of Thomas Aquinas, in his teaching on the sending of the Divine Persons. In *Summa Theologiae*, I, q. 43, Thomas states that a Divine Person, because of his omnipresence, cannot be said to enter a creature since he is already there. Thus we must speak rather of a renewed presence. And since this renewed presence cannot involve a real change in God, it must involve a real change in the creature: a new relationship to the Divine Person. Thence comes a question that charismatics are forced to face: Can one receive the Holy Spirit more than once? To this Thomas would recall that while in baptism we receive the Spirit *simpliciter*, in confirmation we receive a fullness of the Spirit (III, q. 72, a. 2, ad 2). Thus there can be a sending of the Spirit to a person in whom he already dwells in the following way:

> There is an invisible sending [of the Divine Person not only in the initial gift of grace but] also with respect to an advance in virtue or an increase in grace. . . . Such an invisible sending is especially to be seen in that kind of increase of grace whereby a person moves forward into some new act or some new state of grace: as, for example, when a person moves forward into the grace of working miracles, or of prophecy, or out of the burning love of God offers his life as a martyr, or renounces all his possessions, or undertakes some other such heroic act (*Summa* I, q. 43, a. 6, ad 2).

Note that when he gives examples of these "new acts or states of grace" he does not speak of confirmation or holy orders, but rather of miracles and prophecy *et al.*, which fall into his category of "charismatic" rather than "sacramental graces." This is to say that the Pentecostal experience of charismatic activity need not be interpreted merely in relation to baptism and confirmation, but is rather an experience of the Holy Spirit given not so much as an actuation but more as a *gratia gratis datae.*[44]

Baptism in the Spirit is not simply a private affair, a me-and-God experience. It involves the entire Christian community and has for its end not only the growth of the individual but also and perhaps more importantly the edification (up-building) of the community.

> The baptism of the Holy Spirit is not magic, nor is it an isolated religious experience. It is a direct consequence of the birth, death and resurrection of Jesus. . . . To pray for the baptism in the Holy Spirit is to join with the local community and the whole Body of Christ in asking Jesus to release his power in our lives.[45]

Hence the most common context (though hardly necessary or required) for being baptized in the Spirit is among the believing Christian community, praying for that very purpose, often with the community laying hands (that ancient gesture of prayer and concern) on the one being prayed for.[46]

2. Spiritual Gifts

"The Spirit is inseparable from his gifts,"[47] says

Cardinal Suenens. Every Christian has received the Spirit, and hence every Christian has received Spiritual gifts. Gifts such as he gives are not mere objects to be received, but are reflections of the one who gives, turning attention away from the gift and toward the giver. But just as the Spirit is not yet fully visible in each Christian (that is to say, we all need to grow some yet), neither are all his gifts fully visible or manifest. Spiritual gifts are of many kinds and varieties, meant to fill every need of the community, and each for the purpose of building up that community, as is indisputably clear in 1 Corinthians 12. One author has divided the gifts into three categories: teaching gifts, sign gifts, and revelational gifts.[48] Others have called them ordinary or extraordinary, and some have made other divisions. But such divisions are contrived and serve little more purpose than learning aids. Yes, Paul makes mention of certain gifts in his letters, but his lists are far from complete (Rom. 12; 1 Cor. 12). For all gifts are "the concrete realization of divine grace"[49] for the ultimate purpose of building up the community. No further distinction needs to be made.

These gifts are called charisms. What are charisms? Thomas Aquinas refers to a charism (*donum*) as a grace given primarily and directly, not to sanctify the recipients themselves but to help them bring others to union with God. As examples he refers to the gifts mentioned by Paul in 1 Corinthians 12 and Romans 12. In his treatment of the division of grace into sanctifying and gratuitous grace, he says:

And thus there is a two-fold grace—one

whereby people themselves are united to God, and this is called "sanctifying grace"; the other is that whereby someone cooperates with another in leading that person to God, and this gift [*donum*] is called "gratuitous grace," since it is bestowed on someone beyond the capability of nature, and beyond the merit of the person. But whereas it is bestowed on human beings, not to justify them, but rather that they may cooperate in the justification of another, it is not called sanctifying grace. And it is of this that the apostle says (1 Corinthians 12:7): "And the manifestation of the Spirit is given to every person for the common good," i.e., of others.[50]

Much like Thomas Aquinas, Arnold Bittlinger, a German ecumenist and member of the Core Team in dialogue between the Vatican and the charismatic renewal, defines a charism as

. . . a gratuitous manifestation of the Holy Spirit, working in and through, but going beyond, the believer's natural ability for the common good of the people of God.[51]

Both men show clearly that charisms are not merely humanity's doing, but are the Spirit working through human instrumentality, not so much for the purpose of building up the recipient of the charism, but rather for the purpose of building up others, that is, the beholder's community. A charism is not to be seen, though, as a radically new bestowal on the recipient, for, as Thomas said, it is given to persons "beyond" (*supra*) their natural capabilities, not "in spite of" or "outside of."[52]

Theologians and exegetes [within the renewal]
. . . tend to see the charisms as a new dimension of the life of the community under the
power of the Spirit. The newness, however, is
not found in the giving of a radically new capacity, but rather in the elevation, inspiration, in-
fusion with the power of the Spirit of a capacity
which belongs to the fullness of humanity. . . .
Many in the renewal would wish to point out
the danger of over-supernaturalizing the
charisms, as though each manifestation of the
Spirit constituted something miraculous. On the
other hand, all would also warn against a conception of the gifts which would see them purely
as expressions of a psychological state, or as
fulfilling only some sociological function.[53]

Charisms are gifts from God, no matter how one
explains them.

Because modern ears are perplexed by such a
manifestation, the charism of praying in tongues has
received much more attention than it deserves, even
though Paul considers it the least of all the gifts (1
Corinthians 13). George Montague, editor of the
Catholic Biblical Quarterly, has done an excellent
scriptural study on tongues. He sees no New Testament evidence that shows it to have been an ecstatic or trance-like rapture, but rather he regards it as
a pre-conceptual form of prayer. It was a gift (1)
directed toward God, (2) and done under the influence of the Holy Spirit, but (3) it was not the miraculous production of unlearned human language. It
was ordinarily (not extraordinarily) available to
Christians and desirable. This scriptural model, as
he sees it, is a definite biblical precedent for the gift

as it is experienced in the Church today.[54] Montague himself prays in tongues.[55]

Some have attempted to discredit tongues as a pathological condition, or at least the product of unstable personalities. "This is not the view of solid scientific investigation," says Cardinal Suenens, "nor is it that of one of the most qualified men in his field, William J. Samarin, professor of anthropology and linguistics at the University of Toronto."[56] The professor's long international study of tongues said that it contains nothing abnormal or pathological, and he offers proofs.[57]

Tongues is a gift for prayer. Its desirability is obvious because it helps one to pray better.

> There is considerable spiritual value in having a pre-conceptual, non-objective way of praying. . . . Under the power of the Spirit the believer prays freely without conceptual forms.[58]

Its inherent value is that it builds up the one who prays, bringing him beyond overly intellectual forms in a manner similar to the rosary.[59] Its unearthly beauty is often inspiring. The ultimate gift, though, is to the community: the gift of a deeper prayer.[60]

Another charism deserving attention here, and apparently much more esteemed by Paul (1 Corinthians 14:1f) is prophecy. Prophecy is the gift wherein a person, sensitive to God's will, speaks out the mind of God to encourage or admonish the community and the individuals therein. It, too, is a gift given to build up both the individual and the community. While all charisms are for this purpose, this is the special task of prophecy. The Malines Document is clear in explaining it:

The charism of prophecy belongs to the ordinary life of the local church and should not be
looked upon as an unusual grace. Authentic
prophecy proclaims God's will and God's word,
and focuses God's light on the present. Prophecy exhorts, warns, comforts, and corrects, and is
directed to the up-building of the Church (1
Cor. 14:1-5). Extreme care is used with both
predictive and directive prophecy. Predictive
prophecy is not to be acted on except as tested
and confirmed in other ways.

As with all gifts, prophetic utterance can
vary in quality, power, and purity. . . . For this
reason all prophecies are not to be understood
or received at the same level. . . . Prophecies
are to be submitted to the Christian community
[for testing]. . . . They are also submitted to
those who have pastoral responsibilities.[61]

There are many other important spiritual gifts
that cannot be discussed in this work. Many of them
are mentioned in Paul as cited above; some are not.
Among them are interpretation of tongues, healing,
words of wisdom or knowledge, teaching, discernment of spirits, faith and miracles, and administration.[62]

3. Charismatic Spirituality

"The theological basis of the Catholic charismatic renewal is essentially trinitarian,"[63] and so is
its spirituality. God is the Father, approachable only
through his Son Jesus, who having ascended to heav-
en to be with his Father has sent his Holy Spirit to

teach us and guide us to the Father through Jesus.

> It is the reception of the Spirit which incorpo-
> rates one into the body of Christ and makes a
> person a Christian. . . . It is the Spirit who
> constitutes the Church as the body of Christ.[64]

The initial thrust of charismatic renewal is a "personal conversion to Jesus and radical expectancy of
the power of the Spirit,"[65] which leads one ultimate-
ly to union with the Father. It is a

> . . . move toward fullness of life in the Holy
> Spirit, the exercise of the gifts of the Spirit,
> which is directed toward the proclamation that
> Jesus is Lord to the glory of the Father.[66]

One could also describe the charismatic renewal's theological focus as christological, as does Cardinal Suenens.[67] But whether one calls it trinitarian
or christological, the charismatic renewal is based in
the heart of the great mystery of God.

Charismatic renewal has sometimes been ac-
cused of being anti-intellectual. This was often true
of classical Pentecostals, and is even true today in a
few improperly directed elements of charismatic renewal in the Catholic Church. But this does not seem
to be true of most Catholic charismatics, especially
because many Catholic charismatics have, in fact,
come from and remain in intellectual circles. Catholic charismatics are not anti-intellectual. But they do
have other dimensions to their faith besides the intellectual dimension. Faith is not only an acceptance of
doctrinal propositions, but is also and primarily an

adherence to our God who continually reveals himself to us.

> Faith is a living encounter with a living God; it is formulated in the Church within the context of experience. . . . Experiencing Christ comes of necessity before the definition of that experience.[68]

This is the biblical view of humankind, that is, that the knowledge of God originates in the experience of him. This is precisely what is happening today in the charismatic renewal. It is a renewal of the experience of God. This in no way degrades the intellectual dimension of religion, but instead it balances it and enhances it. Charismatic renewal communities not only crave to know about Jesus, but they desire the very experience of his presence. And it is this experience of the presence of Jesus in the power of the Spirit that leads them to proclaim, in the most biblical sense of the word "proclaim," that Jesus is Lord to the glory of the Father.[69]

What is perhaps the most distinguishing characteristic of Catholic charismatics is their expanded awareness of what they received when they were initiated into the Christian community. The scholastic doctrine of *ex opere operantis* points out that we receive according to the degree of our openness. To the degree that a person is open to the gifts and guidance of the Spirit, to that degree and not ordinarily beyond that degree will that person receive the gifts and guidance of the Spirit. Since the baptismal heritage of the sons of God is this Spirit, one's expanded awareness of the depth and breadth of that heritage cannot but help result in greater openness to the Spirit.

For most, if not all Christians, growth is usually slow. Giant steps forward are prized but not frequent. This also is true in Catholic charismatic renewal. Growth is slow, yet there definitely seems to be growth. Hindsight especially reveals remarkable growth among people associated with this renewal. And perhaps most important of all is that people seem to be growing in their faith. This is the "key to understanding this whole spiritual renewal: it is a renewal of faith."[70] From this spring of faith have emerged many rivers of growth, especially in the areas of freedom and dignity, interpersonal relationships, hunger for religious experience, actuation of the laity, ecumenism, social justice, liturgical involvement, and biblical appreciation and study.[71]

Some have claimed that Catholic charismatics are anti-institutional. Such claims are not easily proven. In fact, only the opposite comes close to the truth, for the renewal's effect

> . . . has generally been to give people a greater
> love and appreciation for all that is authentically traditional in the Church.[72]

Some good examples of this are renewed appreciation of all of the sacraments, devotion to Mary, and a respectful and loving attitude of obedience to the authority of clergy and hierarchy.

4. Prayer Meetings

One of the chief elements of charismatic renewal as it is manifested in the Church today is the prayer group or prayer meeting. In Matthew it is written that "if two of you agree about anything on earth in prayer, it shall be granted," and "where two or three are gathered together in my name, there am I in the midst" (Mt. 18:19-20). In the very beginnings of Christianity the experience of the Lord in group gatherings was of the utmost value and importance, whether it was for the breaking of bread or not. It is therefore more than fitting; it is necessary for Christians to gather. It is only logical, then, that a renewal guided by the Spirit would contain the element of gathering to pray, or prayer meetings.

There are two purposes for prayer meetings. The first and most important is to praise and worship God. The second is the direct result of the first, that is, to build up the body of Christ. The prayer meeting focuses on God. The gathered people worship him with song, and in prayer both quietly and aloud glorify his name. Persons present wait for the urging of the Spirit within to empower their prayer and worship. The body of Christ is built in the loving exchange of shared faith, of witness, by teaching, and by the experience of the spiritual gifts.[73]

Prayer groups vary greatly in size, some as small as three or four, some as large as five hundred or a thousand. But the most common size seems to be from twenty to forty. Each group is unique. And if each group is operating as guided by the Spirit, it will manifest the direction for which it is intended, even though these directions or goals may differ quite a bit from group to group, as the Spirit blows, such as, for example:

The Lord does not necessarily intend all such
groups to have a very long existence. He has a
purpose for each group. Some groups, for in-
stance, are only meant by God to exist long
enough to introduce some people to a deeper
life in the Spirit. Some groups may only be intended to exist long enough to give birth to a
group that the Lord does want to develop. Our
concern should not be to prolong the existence
of our group, but to serve the Lord. If the
Lord's purpose for our group is over, we should
move on the way he wants us to.[74]

The atmosphere at the prayer meeting is free,
flexible, quite spontaneous, and full of sensitivity to
the Lord's direction in the community. People pray
together, not just simultaneously. There is no fixed
formula or program that meetings follow, though
some skeletal patterns do tend to develop. Even
though they are spontaneous, prayer meetings are
not wild or chaotic. They proceed peacefully and in
good order, and are usually not too long, which is
good Catholic style. The atmosphere is loving, thus
allowing persons to shed their masks, to pray, and to
share in a genuinely human way.[75] James Byrne has
offered a rather good description of what takes place
in a prayer meeting. He says that it is not a Scripture discussion or a sensitivity session, nor is it even
an event where people do all the sharing. It is a
meeting with the Lord, and in the Lord, and for the
Lord. Meetings are not intended to provide emo-
tional uplifts or social contacts, but are to build up a
mature Christian community. Meetings are subject
to the wisdom of Paul's directions to the Corinthians
(1 Cor. 14:26-33).

At the prayer meetings, someone may share an

event which has happened during the week, another a text from Scripture, another a prophecy, another a song, and so on. The only "rule" is that all things should be done to edify—for the common good. This means that one ought not to speak lightly, but should pray first and try to speak prayerfully. Frequently the prayer meetings will include inspired preaching or a prepared teaching. Everyone is free to speak, but no one is expected to. The attitude in which one should approach a prayer meeting is in readiness to come and see and hear about the good things that the Lord is doing and saying among his people today.[76]

Oftentimes at a prayer meeting a leader will ask for a "word of prayer." A word of prayer is a few moments during which all present pray together, each however he or she wishes. Some will pray quietly, some aloud, some in quiet song, some in tongues. It oftentimes becomes a heavenly symphony of prayer, a beautiful and pleasing prayer to God.

Sometimes during, but most often after the prayer meeting, people will gather in a small group to pray with one or the other person for a particular intention. This kind of prayer context is frequently employed when a person wishes to be baptized in the Spirit, to pray about a decision, to ask for strength in a situation, to ask for healing, to intercede for particular needs, etc. A common gesture used by those praying with the person is the laying on of hands. This gesture is a sign of blessing, of human warmth, of concern, of petition, of delegation, and of spiritual unity. It is a prayer action that reflects a highly scriptural meaning.[77]

The leader's role in a prayer meeting varies with

the nature of the group. Sometimes there is one leader, but more often the leadership is shared by several persons. Their role is simply to facilitate prayer. They might make suggestions regarding readings, prayer forms, themes, and the use of gifts, but in all cases they are responsible for discerning the Lord's will in what they do, lest they find themselves exercising their own leadership rather than the Spirit's. Sometimes they are led to exercise authority in order to correct an abuse, but again a sensitive discernment dominates.[78]

The prayer meeting is seen in no way as a substitute for the Eucharist, the central gathering for all Christians. It is, on the contrary, related to the Eucharist as a continuation of the body formed at Eucharist and as a supplement that both nourishes and is nourished by the Eucharist. It is a gathering of the eucharistic community.

5. The Place of Charismatic Renewal in the Church

There are some figures available that may help us to assess the growth and scope of charismatic renewal in the Catholic Church today. In 1967 there were only a handful of people involved with charismatic renewal. A recent University of Chicago study, however, shows that roughly 2,000,000 American Catholics have attended at least one charismatic prayer meeting, and that approximately 500,000 Catholics around the world, including many priests and religious, attend prayer meetings regularly. In its first four years of life, *New Covenant,* a monthly magazine published for charismatic renewal, expanded to a circulation of 60,000. These are signs of expansion at a significantly high rate, and there are presently no signs of plateauing.[79]

Some are threatened by these numbers. They fear losing control of such a large group, or they fear schism. Such fears are understandable but not well founded. Charismatic renewal is not seeking to become a self-contained movement or a society within the Church or even outside the Church. Like the liturgical renewal, it exists only for the Church. Those who have found themselves in national leadership roles (they prefer to call them "service roles") are keenly aware of this:

> In all things, we have to realize that the charismatic renewal is not the Church. It can never be an end in itself, nor a substitute for the Church. It is a tool for Church renewal. The Church, not the charismatic renewal, is the source of the full sacramental life. It is primarily the Church, and not the charismatic renewal by itself, that is the source of the full and authentic teaching of Christ.[80]

With different words, Kevin Ranaghan, a well-known national leader in charismatic renewal, describes more specifically the role of charismatic renewal in the Church:

> The charismatic renewal in the Catholic Church is the expression or embodiment of a movement on the part of Almighty God for the purpose of charismatically renewing the Church. It is a renewal of the fullness of the gift of the Holy

Spirit on every level of Catholic life, especially imparting lively faith in Jesus, a lively sense of worship, and the gifts and ministries of the Holy Spirit. Therefore the charismatic renewal is not an end in itself nor can it have an existence separate from that of the Church. Rather, the charismatic renewal is part of the Church and exists for the renewal of the Church. Thus the resources, spiritual energies, and the very lives of individuals and communities in the Catholic charismatic renewal are to be laid down in service for the well-being of the whole Church.[81]

The renewal is not a technique, a program, a movement, or a method. "The charismatic renewal consists essentially in a turning to God to await the fullness of his promises."[82] This renewal is a renewal of the most basic tenets of Christianity. It is no exaggeration, then, to say that the charismatic renewal is for all Catholics, all Christians. It is wrong, though, to say that all Christians must attend charismatic prayer meetings or that all Catholics must pray in tongues. But it is not wrong to say that all Catholics and all other Christians must be open to the fullness of the Holy Spirit. Must all Catholics identify with the charismatic renewal? To the extent that it might become a movement in and for itself, no. But inasmuch as it becomes a generic renewal of the Church's cooperation with the working of the Holy Spirit, by all means, yes. To reject the Holy Spirit is the greatest sin of all, the unforgivable sin, for to do so would cut one off from the very life of God, and ascribe the work of Jesus to some other lord (Mk. 3:29).

The long-term goal of charismatic renewal is to phase itself out. The renewal will have no more need or purpose when the Church is renewed, that is, when all the members of the Church are experiencing full life in the Spirit.[83] This goal is obviously some time away from fulfillment. Stephen Clark, another national leader, speaks perceptively to this and other goals in his recent *Where Are We Headed?* Here are some of the goals he lists:

(A) Our goal should not be to have a Catholic Pentecostal movement, but to have a complete renewal of Christian life in the power of the Spirit.

(B) We should move from being identified as "Pentecostals" to being identified as Christians who are discovering how to live and serve "in the Spirit."

(C) We should understand what is happening among us as a renewal rather than as a movement.

(D) The international movement for charismatic renewal should evolve from being a specialized movement to a movement for the restoration of full Christian life.

(E) For a while to come, there should be groups and meetings whose primary focus is charismatic renewal.

(F) We should move from forming groups whose primary focus is charismatic renewal toward shouldering the day-in, day-out work of nurturing Christian life.[84]

The concern is not that people join a movement.

Rather, the concern is that people join God. Joining God means joining the Church he has given in his Son Jesus, and it means accepting the gift of the Spirit he gives to those who are baptized into that Church.

At least one leader feels that the next step for charismatic renewal is "the restoration of disciplined, committed, and successfully functioning Christian communities."[85] He sees charismatic renewal as little more than a warm-up for the struggle of reinstating the basic unit of Christian life, the Christian community.

So far the Catholic Church has not made any dogmatic statements regarding its charismatic renewal. In other words, Catholics are free to decide to participate or not. There have been, however, a significant number of statements made on several levels of authority. One of the earliest pronouncements was a report submitted to the U.S. Catholic bishops by their Committee on Doctrine in 1969. This was not an official position, but nevertheless a result of the Committee's careful study. The main points of the statement were: (1) recognition of the reactionary fears of some against the renewal, (2) specifically calling it a "renewal" and not a "movement," (3) admission that theologically and biblically the renewal has legitimate reasons for existence, (4) seeing the need for further study, (5) urging judgment on the basis of its fruits, which initially seem good in spite of some abuses, (6) concluding that it should be allowed to develop, much in the spirit of Gamaliel, recommending that bishops encourage prudent priests to become involved.[86]

A report was given by Bishop John Quinn to the N.C.C.B. in April 1972 as it assembled in Atlanta. It was quite positive, encouraging bishops to oversee the renewal and asking priests to participate. It also warned against four possible abuses: emotionalism, anti-intellectualism, ecumenical indifferentism, and gnosticism. In reflecting on the disposition of the bishops in Atlanta, Bishop Joseph McKinney, Auxiliary of Grand Rapids, stated: "I would guess that ninety percent of the bishops have the impression that the Catholic charismatic renewal is a good thing in the Church; a few are enthusiastic and some others would like to know more."[87]

A second report was made to the N.C.C.B. by its Pastoral Research and Planning Committee; it was revised and issued by the N.C.C.B. in January 1975, entitled *Statement on Catholic Charismatic Renewal*, and published by the U.S.C.C. The statement began by quoting Vatican Council II's declaration that the Holy Spirit

. . . distributes special graces among the faithful of every rank. . . . These charisms, whether they be the more outstanding or the more simple and widely diffused, are to be received with thanksgiving and consolation, for they are especially suited to and useful for the needs of the Church. Extraordinary gifts are not to be rashly sought after, nor are the fruits of apostolic labor to be presumptuously expected from their use. Judgment as to their genuineness and proper use belongs to those who hold authority in the Church and to whose special competence it belongs, not indeed to extinguish the Spirit, but to test all things and hold fast to that which is good.[88]

The statement urged that the renewal be judged by its fruits, the most authenticating sign of the Spirit being love, accompanied by bearing witness to Jesus. The statement offered hope that these signs are present in the renewal, but also cautioned against the dangers of elitism and biblical fundamentalism. It again strongly urged the involvement of priests and also mentioned prudence in dealing with ecumenical groups. Its final word was: "We encourage those who already belong and we support the positive and desirable directions of the charismatic renewal."

Pope Paul VI has made several statements concerning charismatic renewal. The most noteworthy was his address to the 1975 International Conference on Charismatic Renewal in Rome. On May 19, before over ten thousand people, he made these observations. He first noted the desire of the Catholic charismatic renewal to be situated in the Church, an authentic sign of the Holy Spirit's direction. He said that nothing is more necessary than this renewal which the Holy Spirit is evoking. He asked the people in this renewal to keep in mind three directives that are found in Paul: (1) that they be faithful to the authentic doctrine of the faith, (2) that they accept all spiritual gifts with gratitude, and (3) that they hold love in the highest position because it alone makes the Christian perfect. He urged faithfulness to the sacraments, especially those of the Eucharist and reconciliation, and stressed the necessity of a relationship with the entire Church community to keep them from self-deception. In a later informal comment he said, "It will be very fortuitous for our times, for our brothers, that there should be a generation, your generation of young people, who shout out to the world the glory and the greatness of the God of Pentecost."[89]

Other bishops have made rather encouraging remarks to charismatic renewal groups. In the August 1972 *New Covenant*, Archbishop James Hayes of Halifax noted the deep love for the Church found in charismatic renewal groups. He also said:

> My contact with the charismatic renewal has given me great hope for the renewal of the Church. I see within it some of the elements of the new, wholly new, Pentecost that Pope John announced and prayed for more than a decade ago. I am firmly and strongly convinced that the leaders of the charismatic renewal in the States are really instruments of the Lord in renewing his people here and now. We will see that new Pentecost in the Roman Catholic Church.[90]

At a June 1975 gathering of about six hundred priests involved with charismatic renewal at Steubenville, Ohio, Bishop John Mussio of Steubenville observed that it is not fair to the Church to deprive it of this great work of the Holy Spirit because of the uncontrolled emotions and derogatory remarks of a few. He noted that the evils of the world like materialism can only be overcome by prayer to the Holy Spirit, and he strongly stated: "The charismatic renewal covers the same territory as does the loving Spirit of God." At the same gathering, Bishop Paul Anderson of Duluth remarked: "Charismatic renewal is not a movement. It is the Church coming alive."

In their various statements the bishops have enumerated several cautions or dangers regarding charismatic renewal, and there are others as well. Some cultural baggage has crept unwantedly from classical Pentecostalism into various Catholic groups. It has come in the form of biblical fundamentalism and lack of proper perspective regarding the spiritual gifts, sometimes referred to as "charismania." Insisting on the literal interpretation of Scripture, rashly seeking the spiritual gifts, and insisting that tongues and prophecy are necessary manifestations of the Spirit in each individual are all clearly contrary to Catholic teaching and must be carefully and deftly sliced from the Catholic charismatic package.

Another danger frequently cited is elitism. The elitist is the one who says: "I've got the Spirit; you don't." This attitude shows a narrow understanding of the Spirit. It is true that charismatic groups almost universally tend to germinate spiritual gifts. That is only natural and expected, and it's only too natural for persons to express their joy about it. But not to recognize the presence of the Spirit in the other organs of the Christian body is not only blind, it is sinfully snobbish and could lead to gnostic schism. Unfortunately it has begun to occur in a few places. There is a need for sound guidance in each charismatic group.

Other dangers cited in various places are illuminism—falsely claiming to be directed and enlightened by God; paraclericalism—lay persons try-ing to imitate functions proper to the ordained clergy; emotionalism—excessive or exclusive employment of emotions in religious expression; anti-intellectualism—exclusion of the rational processes from genuine religious activity; ecumenical indifferentism—the naive joining of different religious denominations without regard for their individual traditions; and anti-institutionalism—rejection of the institutional dimension of the Church. None of these seem to be very prevalent or as threatening as the above three, but nevertheless they must not be pushed aside and forgotten. If they are, they may well become dangerous.[91]

One final item deserves treatment here. That is the area of ecumenical concerns. It is true that there is only one Lord, one faith, one baptism, one Father, and one Spirit who works in us all. This is the basis of all ecumenical unity, which will hopefully one day express itself in a common profession of faith and a common eucharistic celebration. The circumstances of the day, however, show that we are not there yet, and that we do have differing traditions. To deny this fosters ecumenical indifferentism and a false unity that can only result in the destruction of all the beautiful traditions. One must never compromise that which is true. Sometimes charismatic groups who include more than Catholics soft-pedal their differences in the name of this false unity. A more proper goal to reach for would be the common respect of each other's traditions rather than a denial of them. Ecumenical contacts obviously require the guidance of those who know professionally what is proper to accept and what is proper to reject.[92]

Rather than being a source of abrasion, charismatic renewal is potentially a healing salve for the festering wounds of division between Christians. It is a drive to pray together, to worship and praise together. It is an encouragement to learn new attitudes and approaches from each other, a place to give great gifts to each other. It is a spring from which a brotherhood can arise so that when the days come when differences are resolved there will already be an atmosphere of loving acceptance, ripe for the unity which all Christians desire.[93]

2
The Council and the Role of the Priest

The documents of Vatican Council II contain a rich description of the role of the Catholic priest in the Church community. In the *Decree on the Ministry and Life of Priests*,[94] the focus of this chapter, the council fathers begin by acknowledging that these are days of great renewal within the Church, and that a heavy portion of the responsibility for this renewal lies on the shoulders of priests. "In the renewal of Christ's Church tasks of the greatest importance and of ever-increasing difficulty are being assigned to this order" (n. 1). This renewal demands a quality in priests that in recent decades has not been as necessary as it is now: adaptability, the ability to maneuver the vessel in the mixing currents of the Spirit and the modern age. In response to this need, the fathers have written their decree for the express purpose of advising priests in their adaptation to this new age of the Church, for "the pastoral and human circumstances of the priesthood have in many instances thoroughly changed" (n. 1). The council fathers have, then, raised up as a model the priest who is able and ready to adapt his ministry to the changing needs of his people:

Where there is need, they [priests] are ready to
undertake new pastoral approaches under the
lead of the loving Spirit who breathes where he
will (n. 13).

This chapter is divided into two parts. In them
are briefly discussed some important matters that
the fathers have raised regarding the priest's relationship to the body of Christ and his function within
the body.

I

RELATIONSHIP TO THE BODY

The council fathers were clear in stating that the
priests hold a position of authority in the body of
Christ. Their authority comes from Christ and
through the bishop, establishing them as fathers and
shepherds among the people of God. Yet the fathers
have placed new emphasis on the role of the priest as
a brother among brothers (n. 9). In the brotherhood
of Christians, every single person is by baptism
entrusted with the up-building of the body. Among
these brothers there are the priests who have their
own particular role in this up-building of the body.
They are "set apart" and yet "within the midst" of
the people of God. The priest may not conform to
the world, but he must nevertheless be deeply involved in the human condition.

They [priests] cannot be ministers of Christ
unless they are witnesses and dispensers of a life
other than this earthly one. But they cannot be

of service to men if they remain strangers to the life and conditions of men (n. 3).

A priest is not above humankind, but is himself a man, a real man among the people of God. If being a human means laughing and singing, then he must laugh and sing. If it means raging, then he must be enraged. If it means crying in the depths of loneliness, then he must cry. He is a man who like all humans becomes frustrated, needs friends and companionship, enjoys the sight of God's created beauty, sins and needs forgiveness, and needs both to love and to be loved. And not less than all of these, a priest is a man who, like every person on earth, needs God. He needs prayer, the sacraments, and a deep personal relationship with God. For it is from this relationship that he derives the meaning of his existence, the salvation of his life, and learns the very purpose for his ministry to the body of Christ.

In the midst of his humanity, a priest must be able to bring the Lord to the people of God. To do this it is presumed that he knows the Lord. Thus he must be deeply absorbed into a full appreciation of his own sacraments of initiation, wherein he has become a full participator in the life-functions of the body (n. 2). He must continually increase his ability to be led by the Holy Spirit in his vocation, in his works of charity, in his human freedom, and in his own growth in faith (n. 6). He must be holy, for God's priestly instruments cannot help but be more effective instruments if they reflect a growing degree of holiness:

Ordinarily God desires to manifest his wonders

through those who have been made particularly docile to the impulse and guidance of the Holy Spirit (n. 12).

It is holiness that opens a priest to the activity of the Holy Spirit. As a means to this holiness, a priest must be fully acquainted with the transforming Word of God in the Holy Scriptures. In doing this he carries out his bishop's mandate to "believe what you read, teach what you believe, and practice what you teach."[95] Therefore, as the council fathers suggest, he "should every day read and listen to that Word" (n. 13). Not only because it is an essential source of spiritual growth does a priest read the Word. He reads it also because it is the source from which his priestly ministry takes its start, for he is first and foremost a proclaimer of the Word (n. 2).

II
THE FUNCTION OF A PRIEST

1. To Proclaim the Gospel

First in the list of priestly functions is the proclamation of the Gospel. It is highest in the order of priority. Priests "have as their primary duty the proclamation of the gospel of God to all" (n. 4). There is no other priestly duty more important than this. It is the cardinal duty, the very hinge of presbyterial ministry. It is the revelation of the good news to humankind. Just as Jesus could do no greater than to reveal himself as God, as a lover and saver, so also a priest can do no greater than to continue revealing this same Jesus to the people of God by the proclamation of the Gospel. A priest shares in the revelation of Jesus. In fact, priests "are so configured to Christ the Priest that they can act in the person of Christ the Head" (n. 2).

A priest can proclaim the Gospel of Jesus in both word and in sacrament. In *word* the priest proclaims the Gospel by evangelizing. As evangelists priests have the responsibility of "sharing the gospel truth in which they themselves rejoice in the Lord" (n. 4). It is necessary, then, that priests have come to know and experience the saving power of the Gospel, that they have been led by the Spirit to the point of rejoicing in it, and that they are able to communicate effectively the joy and the power of the Gospel message to the people of God.

At the heart of his duty to proclaim the Gospel is the priest's task "to summon all men urgently to conversion and to holiness" (n. 4). This is the very nature of the Gospel, for those who truly hear the good news of Jesus are called to repent of their sins and reform their lives by striving for that holiness which joins one's spirit to the activity of the Holy Spirit. The priest then must have experienced conversion so that he may have the faith and the ability to lead others to their conversion to the way of the Lord.

In *sacrament* the priest proclaims the Gospel by touching with the saving hand of Jesus the lives of those who receive the sacraments. In each sacrament there is the activity of saving worship. In this saving worship the priest is present to act in the person of Jesus, from whom all sacramental life comes. It is the priest's mediating role, being the agent of faith-experience for those who celebrate the sacraments, that validates and signs the truth of his Gospel proclamation. The good news is truly that God loves his people. Therefore the people's sacramental experience of the love of God is a validating sign of the truth of the Gospel. It is in this way that the sacraments are a necessary part of the proclamation of the Gospel.

The Eucharist is the highpoint of both the Word and the sacramental proclamation of the Gospel. It is "the source and apex of the whole work of preaching the Gospel" (n. 5). It is the symbolic joining of the proclamation of the Word and the sacramental celebration of all that is central to Christian faith. And if it is true, as the fathers suggest, that the ministry of the priest "derives its power and force from the sacrifice of Christ" (n. 2), then that ministry, the proclamation of the Gospel, loses all its power unless it is joined to the sacrifice of Christ. This joining of the Gospel and the sacrifice is precisely what takes place at the commemoration of the Last Supper, the great eucharistic meal. In this the priest joins himself to Christ the priest, who has validated his Gospel message by his own death and resurrection. So the Eucharist lies at the heart of the Gospel proclamation as both its validation and its highest form of expression.

2. To Forge Unity

"The people of God find their unity first of all through the Word of the living God, which is quite properly sought from the lips of priests" (n. 4). As a preacher of the Word, the priest is also concerned for the unity of the body, because the unity of the body is directly dependent on the Word of God for its existence. As the priest proclaims the Word and the people of God listen and grow in their faith, this same faith becomes the hinge of unity. All the people of God rally 'round their Lord in faith.

Implied in his responsibility of proclaiming the Gospel is the duty of a priest to coordinate the charisms of the body. Within the community which he serves there are many gifts, all given by the Holy Spirit for the up-building of the body. As the community's chief forger of unity, the priest must "foster with diligence the various humble and exalted charisms of the laity" (n. 9). A priest helps the people of God discover the great gifts which they have been given by the Holy Spirit. "Those [charisms] are worthy of special attention which are drawing many to a deeper spiritual life" (n. 9). While some are given charisms that are needed for community organization, such as that of administration, the priest should give his greatest efforts to discovering and ordering charisms that bear more directly on the spiritual growth of the community, such as prayer leadership.

It is indeed the priest as a servant of Christ the priest who "joins them [the people of God] together in one body" (n. 2). It is through Christ the head and the one shepherd of the flock that the priest is given spiritual power to exercise this office "for the up-building of the Church" (n. 6). This office of shepherd or pastor includes "formation of a genuine Christian community" (n. 6) which is built around the center of its worship, the Eucharist. The priest is rightly so called the builder of the eucharistic community because it is joined to Christ the priest that he carries on his duty.

In every community there are squabbles and disagreements. Even in the most well-developed Christian communities, because of the weakness of the human condition, there are tensions and arguments. As the forger of unity, the priest at times must assume the role of reconciler. In this role he is to "reconcile differences of mentality in such a way that no one will feel like a stranger in the community of the faithful" (n. 9). The priest celebrates his role as reconciler in its highest form in the sacrament of penance. In his role as reconciler the priest stands again as one united to Christ the priest, who mediates not only the love of God but also the forgiveness of God.

3. To Teach

Just as a mother's milk will not sustain her offspring for all their lives, neither will the initial proclamation of the Gospel be enough to sustain the people of God in their faith. Continued development of the Gospel life is always necessary. The sacraments are a vital element of this continued Gospel living, but another area of great concern is Christian education. The people of God desperately need continued instruction in the matters of faith and its implications for the Christian life. The priest, therefore, in order to complete his ministry of proclaiming the Gospel, must also be a teacher of the faith and doctrine. He is a man who by his words can instruct the people of God and who by his deeds is visible as a living example of the life of faith. The life of a priest, therefore, is not private. His life and his spirituality are public, just as his office is a public office (n. 2).

A priest must not only teach the people of God about their faith and their God, but he must also be able to teach them about themselves and assist them in the maturing of their lives of faith. He

. . . must persuade all to the discharge of the duties of their proper state in life, and bring the saintlier ones to an appropriate exercise of the evangelical counsels (n. 5).

Cast in this role, the priest is a spiritual director, one appointed to teach and guide individuals, groups within the community, and the community as a whole in their growth before the Lord. "Priests should help people see what is required and what is God's will in the great and small events of life" (n. 5). He helps the people of God respond more deeply to the grace of God, clarifying their experiences and beliefs and discerning their progress. He leads them to discover the Spirit praying in them and guiding their lives.

As a teacher, the priest must also be a visionary. He must be willing and able to gather with the people of God, to listen to them and, recognizing their experience, "read the signs of the times" (n. 9). In this way, together with his own charisms that are guided by the Spirit, the priest will be able to gain a prophetic vision of the Lord's plan of salvation for the present age and will be able to guide and direct the body into cooperation with that plan. In this

visionary activity the priest is responsible for apply-
ing "the perennial truth of the gospel to the concrete
circumstances of life" (n. 4). His is the task of making the message of Jesus real and vibrant for the
present age.

4. Unto the Glory of God

The task of the priest is to proclaim the Gospel,
to forge unity among the body, and to teach the people of God. But to what end? What is the purpose of
all this? The council fathers were crystal-clear in
their answer to this question:

> The purpose, therefore, which priests pursue by
> their ministry and life is the glory of God the
> Father as it is to be achieved in Christ. That
> glory consists in this: that men knowingly,
> freely, and gratefully accept what God has
> achieved perfectly through Christ, and manifest
> it in their whole lives (n. 2).

Every priestly activity has for its ultimate purpose
the glory of the Father. Every priestly activity con-
tributes "to the extension of God's glory, as well as
to the development of divine life in men" (n. 2).
Thus, desiring that it be a worthy gift, he prepares
the Kingdom, in union with Christ, for the day when
it will be handed over to the Father.

3
The Role of the Priest
in the Catholic
Charismatic Renewal

The council fathers stated in their Decree[96] that their purpose was to advise priests in their adaptation to the Church of this modern age. Since the Catholic charismatic renewal is becoming a notable force in this modern age of the Church, it is included among those areas of need where priests are asked to be "ready to undertake new pastoral approaches under the lead of the loving Spirit who breathes where he will."[97] Moreover, since the fathers have urged that the Church's priests involve themselves deeply in the renewal of the body, the charismatic renewal, a potentially powerful breeding ground for the renewal of the body, deserves the special attention of priests. One of the fathers, Cardinal Humbertos Medeiros, attempting to urge his priests to give this special attention to charismatic renewal, wrote a special letter to all the clergy of his archdiocese. In that letter he encouraged his priests to provide guidance for prayer groups, to strengthen those elements of charismatic renewal which are of God, and to clarify that which is to be avoided. He also asked his priests to meet with each other regularly for prayer and discussion in the spirit of charismatic renewal.[98]

Cardinal Medeiros' approach characterizes the attitude of the council fathers as it could be applied to the charismatic renewal. But if his attitude and that of the U.S. bishops can be called "urging" priestly involvement, then the attitude among those faithful already involved in charismatic renewal can be called, more strongly, "crying out." This is evident from the following example. A large number (22,000) of the nation's Catholic charismatics were gathered in the football stadium of Notre Dame University at a June 1973 conference for Catholic charismatic renewal. One of the speakers on the platform was addressing the bishops present. He asked the bishops if they would each appoint a priest director for charismatic renewal in his own diocese. The stadium reacted with a standing ovation. Then the speaker asked the bishops to send priests to prayer groups to minister sacramentally. There was another standing ovation. Finally the speaker asked the bishops to themselves take time to come and pray with their people. Once again the crowd stood and cheered with delight. The bishops present were noticeably pleased. Where else in the Church today are people crying so loudly for the leadership of the clergy?[99]

It appears that there is a need for some priests, if not many, to adapt their ministry to serve the needs of the people involved in charismatic renewal. It is to these needs that the rest of this book is addressed. With this prelude, then, begins the practical excursion into the priest's role in charismatic renewal.

I
RELATIONSHIP TO CHARISMATIC RENEWAL GROUPS

1. An Authority Figure

Strong authority figures do not receive overwhelming applause in these modern days of liberty and individualism. Yet it is in just such days as these that the presence of genuine (not autocratic or oppressive) authority is the most necessary. This authority is necessary in order to preserve the Church from fads and mistaken trends, and to keep the Church in the mainstream of its own tradition and the Gospel.

> The Roman Catholic Church today, in the throes of great change, finds that it cannot call into question the authoritarian stance of the Church without real anguish, because that very stance has been the source of no small measure of blessing and strength down through the centuries.[100]

This refers to, of course, authoritarianism in a more benevolent sense, a power marked not by oppression but by service, a charismatic authority given not to all Christians, but only to those who have been ordained to exercise it. This authority is exercised by those who have the office of speaking with the authority of the Lord. All Christians are called to give witness to Jesus, but only the ordained have the specific ministry of speaking in the name of Jesus the servant.

Catholic charismatic renewal groups are commonly known to show great respect for the authority of the ordained. For example, charismatic renewal leaders frequently urge their groups to be open to the leadership of the clergy who have been entrusted with the shepherding of the Church. As one national leader says:

> We must be fully open with our bishops and pastors about what the Lord is doing in this renewal. We must accept their authority, for it comes from Christ. We must accept their correction and advice, trusting the Holy Spirit to work through them. . . . We must also remind our pastors that they have the obligation and grace from God to judge, approve, confirm, and bless the authentic movement of the Lord among his people.[101]

The outcry is for pastors to use the grace and authority they have been given in the Holy Spirit to judge, to whatever extent is possible, the good and the bad within charismatic renewal groups, and to guide the groups toward growth in the Lord.

The presence of a priest with a prayer group, even in a low-key relationship, is vital because the priest is probably "the single most important person for determining what will succeed and what will fail in the parish."[102] This is most important to recognize, especially considering the respect that many Catholics have for the judgment of their priests.

Many Catholics acknowledge this unique role when they seek the pastor's encouragement and endorsement before they will consider becoming personally involved in the charismatic renewal.[103]

Whether or not this is a healthy attitude for Catholics is beyond the scope of the present question. The fact remains that some Catholics operate out of this understanding of the role of the priest in the Church. They need someone who can give a discerning nod of approval when they are hesitant as well as a nod of caution when they are too eager. In other words, they need and deserve the pastoral attention of the Church.

2. A Brother Among Brothers

A priest-centered approach to leadership is contrary to the spirit of ministry in the Church today. The Spirit seems to be guiding the Church of Jesus to develop all of the ministries, especially among the laity where the ministries have lain fallow for too long. As one bishop put it, speaking in the spirit of Vatican II about the various ministerial functions in the Church:

Many of those different functions have been telescoped into the role of the priest. We need to recover the distinction in practice so that we can see the ministry of the Church in its full scope. If our focus is on the minister, we can lose sight of the ministry. It is the whole Church that ministers, but in our present situation the ministry seems to come from the priest. . . . The ministry of the Church needs to be broadened to include more people doing different things in the name of the Church.[104]

This is the direction of the Church. This is also the direction of charismatic renewal within the Church.

In charismatic renewal Catholics are beginning to experience that they are able to be powerful and effective ministers to the body of Christ. They sense being not an audience, but participating members of the Church in grace, in power, and authority given by God. This comes as a result of opening to God in faith and becoming persons who, by God's grace, are becoming spiritually mature in prayer, sacraments, reading Scripture, meditation, and so on. They receive many spiritual benefits (gifts) which they employ to bear good fruit. They have ministries: abilities to teach, counsel, lead people in prayer, preach, heal, and reconcile.

The ministries, then, are not just the things that priests can do. It is a fallacy to say that priests deal with spiritual affairs and the laity with temporal affairs. What a shame it would be to tell lay persons with the gift of leading a group in prayer that they should limit their activity to the temporalities of the group! It is a serious mistake to presume that the priest must be the front-runner in the leadership of a prayer group. While there is no reason why he may not be such, the fact remains that it is often the case that he is not the chief of the chiefs. The priestly ministry is one of leadership, but this is not to deny others the leadership roles that they have been charismatically endowed to perform. For a priest to presume that his is always the last word is to stifle the initiative of the others and perhaps to inhibit the working of the Spirit.[105]

A priest needs to first be a brother, a simple Christian relating to simple Christians. Then and only then can he be a priest to them. The brotherhood of priests does not take spiritual precedence over the brotherhood of the people of God. If he would be a spiritual separatist or would consider himself a member of a spiritual elite, he would be saying in deed that he is above the people of God, not among them. There is a constant, subtle temptation for priests to use the privileges of rank that often accompany the priestly office, and to build relationships on the basis of their professional competence or their status. A priest is first a brother. To be otherwise is distancing; it puts his rank between himself and his people. So if a priest is not the leader of a charismatic prayer group, that is perfectly all right. It is not necessarily the role of the priest to be the leader. His role as a brother in a particular group might even be more to be *ministered to* rather than to minister. Priests need that too![106]

3. Open to the Holy Spirit

Without delving too deeply into the age-old discussion of charism *versus* office, it is necessary to point out that both charism and office are operative in priestly ministry, and often they overlap. Priests are empowered not only by a spontaneous moving of the Spirit, but also by an abiding sacramental (holy orders) grace that is associated with the priestly office. Both the spontaneous and the sacramental graces can be called charisms because they are gifts of the Spirit. But an important difference between them is that the sacramental grace of orders has been institutionalized, whereas the spontaneous grace has not. Neither is any less a charism than the other, and both demand a full openness to the activity of the Holy Spirit to be present and effective.

The charism of the priesthood is a special blessing to the Church and of the utmost importance to the body. It is the priest, speaking in the name of Christ, leading the sacramental celebration of the Church, and proclaiming the good news of Jesus, who is the most effective minister of the sanctification of the people of God. A priest cannot abdicate his charism, as, for example, a healer could refuse forever to pray for healing. A priest can only, by not being docile to the impulses of the Spirit, perform his charismatic office badly. But by believing in the power that he is given, a priest will become a charismatic minister of the Gospel in a way that he could not be alone, for he has a permanent partner working within him—the Holy Spirit.[107]

An important element of openness is knowledge. It is difficult if not impossible for a person to be open to something of which he is not aware. A priest cannot know the Lord without knowing his Word in Scripture. Neither can a priest know the workings of the Spirit in charismatic renewal without learning about the renewal. It is for this reason that it behooves a priest to become informed about the charismatic renewal. He needs to know about the baptism of the Spirit, the gifts of the Spirit, and the spirituality and ecclesial orientations of charismatic renewal in order to be a brother and an effective priest to those in charismatic renewal.

The priest also needs to be open to the transforming activity of the Spirit in his own life. If he senses himself being pulled away from a charismatic group, then he must leave. If he senses the Spirit leading him toward involvement in charismatic renewal, he must take the risk of following. God knows what he is doing far better than people do.

One other element of openness is openness to the gifts that the Spirit gives. Each priest receives out of the love of God not only the charism associated with his office but also other charisms which the Spirit endows in a more spontaneous way. One national leader in charismatic renewal said it this way:

> We must also recognize that our ordained clergy—bishops, priests, deacons—are all meant to have the spiritual gifts for their jobs. We must support them, encourage them, and urge them to yield to the fullness of the specific ministry gifts they have been given by God.[108]

The Spirit gives gifts for the good of the community. It is only reasonable to expect that the Spirit will richly endow those whom he has chosen to be the priests in the midst of the community.

II
THE FUNCTION OF A PRIEST IN CHARISMATIC RENEWAL

1. To Proclaim the Gospel

The Decree stated clearly that priests "have as their primary duty the proclamation of the Gospel of God to all" (n. 4; see note 96). This is no less true in

charismatic renewal groups than it is in the wider
scopes of the whole parish and the entire Church.
The focal point of the priestly ministry in charismatic renewal is the proclamation of the Gospel. From
this fountain all of the priestly functions spring.

Because they are founded on the proclamation
of the Gospel, nearly all charismatic activities are
directed specifically toward building the relationship
of the people of God with their God. Regular prayer
meetings, mutual support, encouragement toward
growth, the charismatic gifts of the Spirit, being
baptized in the Holy Spirit—all of these are means
by which people can deepen in faith and advance in
spirituality. They are developing an atmosphere of
community in which growth is enkindled. And what
is more, in all this they glorify the Lordship of Jesus,
because it is from him that this salvation and grace
come. Charismatic groups are quick to recognize
this, which makes all the more understandable their
fluent praise of Jesus.

> The heart of this renewal, then, is not that the
> baptism of the Spirit or charismatic ministries
> be restored to Church life, although that is ex-
> tremely vital. The purpose of the Spirit is that
> the Church see "bringing people to the Lord" as
> its basic mission, learn how to bring this about
> in pastoral care, and direct its preaching to ac-
> complish this goal.[109]

It is from the midst of this Gospel mission that the
priest's functions emerge.

(a) *To Evangelize.* It is the priest who stands at
the center of the mission of "bringing people to the

Lord," for it is his primary commission in the body of Christ to be the proclaimer of the Gospel. He is responsible for the telling of the Good News in the Church. He is the evangelizer. He shares his own faith experience and the experience of the Church with those who have ears to hear. He thus summons people to conversion and holiness and leads the community to rejoice with him in that faith.

It is in the very activity of evangelizing that the mission of charismatic renewal and the mission of the priesthood in the Church join into one. United in their faith in the Gospel of Jesus, both the priesthood of Jesus and the charismatic renewal stand amid the Church community to proclaim the salvation brought about in the paschal mystery of Jesus, as well as the promise of eternal life to believers. United not only in faith, both are also united in their desire to provide the pastoral care necessary for the faithful to grow in the Gospel faith and for them to accept the Lordship of Jesus. The priest as an individual united to Christ and the charismatic renewal as a community united to Christ are complements in the proclamation of the Gospel. The charismatic renewal communalizes priestly activity; the priest personifies the activity of the charismatic community.

(b) *To Sacramentalize.* As a proclaimer of the Gospel, the priest is not only an evangelizer, he is also a sacramentalizer. He presides in the person of Christ at the saving worship of the Christian community. He is the agent of the faith experience of those who celebrate the sacraments. In this very real way he "brings people to the Lord."

The sacramental life of the Church has sustained this over all the centuries of its existence. While the particular prayer experiences and charismatic gifts associated with charismatic renewal are important in the on-going life of the Church, the experience of sacraments in charismatic renewal groups remains a necessity for the spiritual sustenance of the groups. It is the sacraments that provide them with an objective expression for their subjective fervor and enthusiasm. The sacraments ritualize the heart of their charismatic experience, thus stabilizing and validating that experience.

The sacramental role of the priest in charismatic renewal can hardly be over-emphasized. Standing at the center of the Church's sacramental mode of proclaiming the Gospel is the priest *in persona Christi*. By remaining close to the priest in his sacramental ministry, the charismatic renewal is assured of remaining close to the mainstream of the Church and remaining near to the source that feeds the entire Church.[110] When those involved with charismatic renewal experience the Lord in sacrament, the truth of the Gospel they preach is validated for themselves and for the Church community.

The Gospel and the sacraments: these are inseparable. A genuine renewal of the Church is a renewal in both the proclamation of the Gospel in word and in the experience of the sacraments. This kind of renewal is precisely the goal of the charismatic renewal in the Catholic Church.

2. To Forge Unity

(a) *To Discover and Order Charisms*. Because

a priest is the proclaimer of the Gospel, he is therefore responsible for the unity of the body which depends on that Word for its unity. Implied in this unity-forging is the ordering of the charismatic ministries of the body. As a priest becomes more and more familiar with a charismatic group, he can gradually assume his proper role in that Christian community as coordinator of ministries. Beyond recognizing needs for particular gifts and ministries, and because his duty is to "foster with diligence the various humble and exalted charisms of the laity,"[111] the priest should be able to call forth these ministries from those who are correspondingly gifted to serve. It is the priest's job to encourage and develop ministries in the community.[112]

Since he coordinates their ministries too, a priest should know the leaders of the group well, for several reasons. First, they have been entrusted with a heavy spiritual responsibility and will surely need and likely ask for priestly guidance. Second, since the priest coordinates as a brother among brothers, this needs to be truly the case with the leaders of the brothers, especially when a group is too large for the priest to know everyone personally. It may be the only realistic way for him to make his brotherhood felt. Third, if corrections in doctrine or practice become necessary, it is often much wiser for the priest to work through the leaders rather than risking a disruption of the entire group. Finally, it is often the case that the leaders of a prayer group have themselves been involved with charismatic renewal for a considerable period of time. The priest can learn much from them and he can share with them the ministry of coordinating the gifts and ministries.

In this ministry of coordination the priest is ministering for the Spirit in the strictest sense. It is the Spirit who gives the gifts and ministries to the body through which the body becomes a community of the living Spirit. The priest, in coordinating the gifts and ministries, is no less than a servant to the Holy Spirit, God's "organ-izer."

(b) *To Be a Shepherd.* The love in the ideal shepherd's heart is beyond measure. The shepherd has a consuming love for his sheep. In this love is his success as a shepherd, and without it is his failure. The sheep easily sense whether or not he loves them, and on that basis either trust him and depend on him or do not trust him and refuse to follow him. When the loving shepherd is present the sheep are secure; when he is absent, they are fearful.

There is only one shepherd, the Good Shepherd. Only under his pastoring and in his love are the sheep secure. Yet the Good Shepherd has appointed his priests to be co-shepherds, to carry out a large part of the duty of shepherding. The priest *in persona Christi* is the official shepherd of the Lord's sheep, and he, like the Lord, must have a deep and consuming love in order to be a successful shepherd.

To refer to the people of God as "sheep" is not to be construed as insulting, as if they are dumb animals who have no intelligence of their own. The priest is a shepherd, like the Lord, not in the sense of dominating. This is especially true in charismatic renewal. Instead of viewing his role as one of domination, the priest views his role of shepherd rather as an opportunity to be present among his people, to serve them and minister to them. The sheep in charismatic renewal, as in the whole Church, depend on the Lord for his love, not for his domination.[113]

Ministering to charismatic renewal groups provides a special opportunity for priests. It is essential to the identity of a shepherd who is responsible for the spiritual welfare of his flock to be able to minister in a deeply spiritual way. Because the nature of charismatic groups is expressly spiritual, so is his ministry to that group. It is a chance to be with a group that is neither a committee nor a meeting and to exercise a ministry that is directed specifically toward deep spiritual renewal. The priest can get to know the members of his flock in a deeper and more personal relationship than perhaps ever before. Not only does the priest benefit, but so do the people of God, for their need to be known and loved by the shepherd is no less than the need of the shepherd to know and care for them.[114]

As its shepherd the priest constantly examines the fruits of a charismatic group. Since it is principally by their fruits that they are known, the priest must continually call to the attention of the group those fruits which they have and those which they lack. The shepherd would make a serious mistake if he would not discern the effects that a group has on itself and on the parish. It is his duty to do all that he can to insure that the fruits of the group are only sweet fruits. One important way of doing this is for him to concentrate his care on the leaders of the group, helping them to be open, balanced, and faith-filled Christians. Even if the shepherd cannot know all the sheep, he must at least know and direct those among them who are recognized and respected as leaders.

A shepherd "secures the individual members of

the body of Christ in their personal walk of faith by
a ministry of follow-up."[115] Follow-up is important
in charismatic renewal especially because of the deep
spiritual experiences that accompany it. A shepherd
is willing to speak with a member of the people of
God after that member has had a moving personal
experience or a difficult time, and to provide pastoral care in the name of the Lord. He will also
follow up on a group experience by discussing it with
the leaders of the group and giving feedback from
his own unique vantage point.

A shepherd protects his flock from danger. The
common dangers in charismatic renewal are not
wolves, persecutors that attack from the outside. The
real dangers are mostly internal, where the flock
might be in danger of being led too close to a cliff.
One such internal danger is the presence of a person,
either a leader of the group or not, who like a
bruised apple can eventually spoil the entire bushel.

> A single wrong person is sometimes capable of
> ruining a prayer meeting and even of breaking
> up a community. By his untimely or unspiritual
> remarks he can destroy the movement of the
> Spirit; by his unwise exhortations he can mis-
> lead some and disturb others. He can make
> meetings so unpleasant that many people will
> stop coming to them, or make such a bad im-
> pression on visitors that they will reject the
> whole movement. By turning people against one
> another, he can split the community into cliques
> and factions and thus dissolve it.[116]

A priest can guard against "bad apples" by either

removing them or, preferably, by helping them correct their faults. The entire community has, of course, a responsibility to guard against dangers in a community, but the priest, because he is given the pastoral office of the Church, bears the heavier responsibility of shepherding.[117]

As some of the dangers emerge, the shepherd must often be a reconciler. For example, one of the most threatening dangers in charismatic renewal is that of elitism.[118] Combating this danger demands a reconciliation with the larger Christian community. A pastor, being concerned with "the overall good of the parish and of each member,"[119] can bring to a charismatic group his experience of the faith of the parish and the Church as a whole, showing how it is not only charismatic groups that have faith. Then he can ask the group to beg forgiveness for its self-righteousness. If the group ever again becomes self-righteous, he need only remind them of the other holy people in the parish and how they too share in the life of the Spirit.

Another danger, biblical fundamentalism, must be treated delicately lest a priest slander his Pentecostal brothers in the classical tradition who are the most visible proponents of fundamentalism in charismatic circles today. Usually sound scriptural scholarship, which most shepherds have available to them, is enough to counteract this tendency. This scholarship is especially effective if presented by the priest himself, who can speak in the name of Christ's Church.

Charismania, the tendency to magnify the role of charismatic gifts to a distorted proportion, can be dealt with by showing the gifts in their proper perspective in light of the Gospel values. St. Paul himself is clear on what is passing and what is permanent (1 Cor. 13). Many other dangers such as illuminism, paraclericalism, emotionalism, anti-intellectualism, ecumenical indifferentism, and anti-institutionalism are best handled with a gentle word of correction before they are allowed to grow. If these remain unchecked in their early stages, the shepherd is in danger of having a divided flock or a lost one. Preventive medicine is nearly always the best.

(c) *To Confess One Faith.* The priest forges unity in charismatic renewal not only as an orderer of charisms and as a shepherd, but also as the guarantor of doctrinal unity with the whole Church. The people of God can rightfully expect that their priest knows the doctrines of Christianity and the Catholic tradition well, and that he will not allow the group to stray from these doctrines.

In the instances where doctrinal correction is needed, the priest comes through well if, instead of being dogmatic in his approach, he deals with the matter prayerfully and gently puts it into perspective with the Church's doctrine. Mistakes in doctrine are rarely a matter of ill-will on the part of the mistaken, so these persons should not normally be burned like heretics. A loving and encouraging approach is most sensible and quite effective.

Not every error needs to be corrected by a priest or a leader. Because the Holy Spirit is the guide of a genuine charismatic group, it often happens that doctrinal errors are cleansed in a mysterious way by the workings of the Spirit. They fall by the wayside and blow away without bothering the group. But when people are not open to the direction of the Spirit of truth, they may fall into repeated false doctrines. In such instances it is the priest who can step in and make a loving correction. He can deal gently but firmly and promptly, exercising an authority of which the group as a whole is not capable. Perhaps a good rule of thumb for the priest might be this: Wait until a doctrinal error is repeated two or three times before making a direct correction. In this length of time those who are open to the Spirit can be corrected within themselves, and the delay will keep the priest from appearing to be a dogmatic watchdog of orthodoxy.[120]

(d) *To Build a Eucharistic Community.* It is because he is joined to Christ the priest and Good Shepherd that the priest is rightly called the builder of the eucharistic community. One of the principal pastoral objectives in the Church today is "to build communities which make it possible for a person to live a Christian life,"[121] to create an environment wherein the Gospel can be proclaimed, heard, and acted out. There can be no greater symbol and celebration of this community than the community's eucharistic worship.

Charismatic renewal has had no small effect on the worshiping of its proponents. Many persons involved in charismatic renewal report the refreshing experience of integrating the liturgical reforms commissioned by Vatican II with their new-found spiritual renewal. Thus in charismatic renewal there is evidence of a renewal of not only ritual form but also faith content.

The charismatic renewal of worship in the Christian community issues a strong challenge to bishops and priests who preside at the Eucharist:

Where worship is more than the performance of ritual, leaders will be expected to do more than officiate or preside. This takes more than an administrator or a learned theologian; it takes a humble man of the Spirit. An increasing number of bishops and priests are rising to this challenge. . . . Through the charismatic renewal, many Christians have discovered that all of life is meant to be an unceasing prayer of thanksgiving for God's gift of the Spirit, and that the celebration of the Eucharist is the focal point of this life.[122]

The priest, united with Christ the priest, can allow this to happen by his own cooperation in the mystery of the Eucharist.

If there is no priest associated with a charismatic group, this group might be led into a false decision. They might choose between sacramental and charismatic worship. Despicable as this division may seem, groups who have no priestly guidance can easily forget to integrate their charismatic experience into the worship life of the Church. It is the leaders of the group who bear a large portion of the responsibility in this matter. But as president of the eucharistic community, the priest bears the ultimate responsibility for preventing this mistake from being made.[123]

A charismatic renewal group will either leaven or it will divide the parish; there is little in-between. It always has within it the potential for dividing the parish, even though it is not intended to do so. It is, therefore, the special role of the pastor, the eucharistic forger of unity, to allow the group to be a leaven for the whole parish and to integrate it into the parish community, lest it instead divide the parish. The following rather lengthy quotation from Stephen B. Clark speaks about movements as they enter a parish. Clark illustrates how this dividing or leavening can take place:

> In situation A, a new movement enters a parish. At the beginning, the members feel that in being part of the movement they are helping the Church (because the Church needs this). They enthusiastically take part in the movement and just as enthusiastically (and naively) begin to spread it. They then receive a certain amount of opposition. They find themselves avoided by the pastor. They hear remarks he has made about them. Since most of them are not seasoned veterans of parish activities, they do not know the channels and protocol. They begin to feel alienated from the Church. They feel they have to make a choice between this new set of values with the community they have found through it and the institutions of the Church (the Church is seen by them almost exclusively as an institution and not at all as a community). As some of their members opt for the pastor and the parish, the others harden more and more. If their community is strong enough, they go underground or leave the Church as a group. If their community is too weak to withstand the pressure, the individuals "hang loose" from the institutional Church or leave it altogether. The legacy is hard feelings on all sides.
>
> In situation B also, a new movement enters

a parish. The same sort of enthusiasm is generated both for the new movement and the Church. The same sort of reaction of fear, distrust, and opposition arises among other parishioners. The pastor, however, makes a point of finding out what is going on. He comes to the meetings of those who are part of the new movement in an attempt to understand the experience which is motivating these people. He reads the literature of the movement in an effort to understand how this movement might fit into the life of the Church or the parish. Even before committing himself to a course of action, he begins to talk to the members of the movement about excesses and about situations of difficulty they are causing that they might not be aware of. He brings different groups together to talk about what is happening and what the reactions are. He directs the new group toward a place in the parish and, if he feels the group is making an important enough contribution, he encourages them openly. When the movement dissipates, if it does, there is at least no legacy of hostility toward the Church. If it does dissipate, many members of the movement become workers and leaders in parish activities.

Members of movements rarely have enough experience or vision to know how to integrate themselves into the life of the Church. The Church today is lucky that in a number of movements, which could be potentially the most disruptive, the leadership is in the hands of people who are committed to the overall good of the Church and not just to the set of values fostered by their movements. But it should be even more the role of the pastors within the Church to integrate movements into the Church than it is the role of the leaders of the movements. The pastoral office is the office which is concerned with the overall good of the whole Church (or parish or basic community). The leadership of the movements will most naturally be filled by the people who can most effectively advocate the cause which has given rise to the movement, and they will not be as sensitive or experienced in the problems of integration.[124]

3. To Teach

It was Jerome who said in one of his writings that "whoever is a shepherd must be a teacher." Teaching, because it is so closely associated with the priest's primary duty to proclaim the Gospel, is in word and deed an essential element of his ministry. The priest is not the only or exclusive teacher, yet it is his distinctive office to "go and teach all nations," as was said to the Twelve.

In charismatic renewal there is an appetite for sacred doctrine and for knowledge about their experience of the Lord. The people of God want to know about this experience they are having. It is the priest who should have the Word they seek. This requires of a priest that he be fully aware of his own religious experience. Moreover, the people of God have every right to expect that the priest's religious experience and the truth are the same. In order for this to be so, the priest must have (1) solid theological training, and (2) the grace of God in his Holy Spirit to guide him.

(a) *To Instruct.* "If error sometimes finds its way into Pentecostal groups, this is largely due to the fact that it has encountered a doctrinal vacuum."[125] Experience shows that where there is no teaching, the Church soon deflates. Yet there are some priests who would be reluctant to give instruction to a charismatic renewal group even at their request. Some common reasons offered are that they themselves are not involved with the group, that they are uninformed about the nature of charismatic renewal, or that they are afraid of it. Charismatic groups need instruction just as much as other parish groups, if not more so, and a priest, whether he realizes it or not, is in a good position to give them doctrinal instruction. A priest will probably find the group both grateful and receptive. And in the process of instructing them a priest can not only get to know them better, but also can perhaps help the group make a sound assessment of its direction.

As a teacher of the Church, the priest needs to be careful to teach only what is within the limits of the Church's teaching, not to expound on his own theories and theological systems. Or if he does go beyond the Church's official teaching, he should be sure that his listeners are aware that he is presenting a personal viewpoint. This is especially important to a charismatic community where the group looks to the priest for an affirmation of truth and doctrinal orthodoxy.[126]

There are many areas in which charismatic groups need instruction. In each of these the priest will be more or less (hopefully more) competent. By his theological reflection he should be able in some way to deal with these needs:

(a) Explain "Pentecostal elements" such as baptism of the Spirit and charismatic ministries, in accord with Catholic dogma.

(b) Add the experiences and teaching on prayer and the spiritual life present in Church tradition.

(c) Integrate Pentecostal elements into the people's lives so that other helps given by God are not overlooked or shoved aside (sacraments, doctrinal teaching, moral guidance).

(d) Discern those elements of Protestant Pentecostal teaching which represent a denominational point of view, sometimes incompatible with Catholic doctrine.

(e) Help the people avoid fundamentalism in scriptural interpretation.[127]

With regard to this latter, biblical fundamentalism, it is worth remembering that fundamentalism existed well before modern scholarship. Though a priest may disagree even strongly with that approach, he is still called to large degrees of respect and love for those in the fundamentalist tradition, even if their scriptural interpretations are inaccurate.

Without the teaching of the pastoral leaders of the Church, the charismatic renewal would be in constant danger of separation from the mainstream of Christian life. If such were to actually happen, it would be those same pastoral leaders who would bear a large part of the blame. However, where teaching is fully present, charismatic renewal can be a strong positive force in the renewal of the Church.

(b) *To Give Spiritual Direction.* Both individuals in charismatic groups and the groups themselves need spiritual direction. Many have begun a deep life of prayer and spirituality, and "they need [a priest's] professional guidance to avoid the pitfalls of being overzealous and imprudent."[128] The priest's acquaintance with spiritual writers, pastoral counseling, psychology, and his own personal experiences in spiritual growth all become valuable tools for helping a charismatic group and its members through their growing pains onward toward greater and better things.

In a discussion concerning the priest as a spiritual director in charismatic groups, George Martin, publisher of *New Covenant*, said about spiritual directors:

> A spiritual director helps chart a course toward proper growth in the Christian life. He rarely makes decisions for those he directs; but rather helps others to clarify their spiritual condition and to discern God's will for them.[129]

This is a task that a priest can perform for a prayer group. In order to do it well, though, he will need to be familiar with the group and have a sense of the group and its purpose, and he will need to consult regularly with the leaders of the group.

(c) *To Be a Visionary.* To be a true teacher, the priest must have a broad perspective of the Church. He must be a man of vision. As a man of broad vision, the priest sees much more than a charismatic renewal group in his sights. He sees the entire Church. He will be the one who can paint charismatic renewal into its proper place in the picture of the Church and help the renewal to integrate its work of renewal into the Church. His ministry does not remain exclusively in charismatic groups, but is alive and fresh in all the areas of the Church. He avoids falling into the fallacy that one model of the Church or one model of the charismatic prayer group is *the right model*. He stands for the legitimacy of a plurality of structures. With this as his vision the priest will be able to help guide and direct the charismatic group into cooperation with God's eternal plan of salvation, unto the glory of God the Father.

III
ENTERING CHARISMATIC RENEWAL:
SOME FINAL THOUGHTS FOR PRIESTS

Many priests will, if they haven't already, be faced with the presence of a charismatic renewal group in their parish areas. In investigating this situation, priests might recall how strongly the bishops are urging priests to be involved so that there is sound guidance and correct teaching.[130] They might also recall how anxiously charismatic groups themselves seek the presence of priests among them to guide them. And, finally, they might recall how powerful an instrument the charismatic renewal is as an instrument in the priestly ministry of proclaiming the Gospel to the people of God.

Where there is already a charismatic prayer

group established in a parish, the priest's first step in
dealing with them might best be to contact its leaders, and later the group as a whole. In doing so he
should learn as much as he can about the group and
about charismatic renewal. Some priests will be
tempted to take the stance of Gamaliel: "If this en-
terprise, this movement of theirs, is of human origin
it will break up of its own accord; but if it does in
fact come from God you will not only be unable to
destroy them, but you might find yourselves fighting
against God" (Acts 6:38-39). While this "let them
be" policy might be good for a time and might even
be the wisest approach in the beginning, it is good
only for a time. At some point a priest will have to
take a stand. The only alternative is to never take a
stand and to remain innocuously lukewarm and non-
directive. Perhaps the best approach is the one cur-
rently being used by the bishops of the United
States. From their large-scale perspective, they
began their statements on charismatic renewal in the
spirit of Gamaliel. But they have come to realize
that there is a great need for offering guidance to the
renewal, both positive and negative. The Canadian
bishops have also begun this kind of guidance.[131]
This same employment of guidance is appropriate on
a smaller scale in the local parish. While the priest
may wisely begin with a Gamaliel approach, he dare
not perpetuate it. He will eventually need to take a
discerning position regarding his local charismatic
prayer group. He can encourage what is good, and
he can guide toward growth that which needs im-
provement. Or, if the group would be harmfully out
of line with Christian principles, he may after careful
thought and deep prayer need to stand as opposed to

the group. However, in any case, the priest must eventually develop a definite and public posture toward the charismatic group.[132]

A priest need not feel obliged to immerse himself fully into the charismatic renewal in order to give sound pastoral guidance to a charismatic group. He needn't be "baptized in the Spirit" to aid others in their dealings with the Spirit. His simple presence as a pastor can in itself do a great deal of good, and is sufficient for providing basic pastoral care for the group.

After some time of involvement with a charismatic renewal group, a priest might wonder whether or not he should be more than an observer-advisor and perhaps commit himself to the renewal in a deeper way. In such a case, if he chooses this deeper personal involvement, then he needs to rediscern what his proper role in the group should be: simple member, part of the leadership, advisor, or whatever. Two pitfalls for a priest to avoid in discerning this question are these: On the one hand, for a pastor to simply "take charge" of a group can be a mistake, because, as is now true in most aspects of Church life, team ministry is the more advisable form of leadership. On the other hand, the need for strong pastoral involvement is clear, so to withhold this kind of care would be just as much a mistake as "taking over."[133]

Epilogue

When all is said and done, how does a priest answer this question: "What is the real purpose for my ministry to a charismatic renewal group?" To answer this question, the priest would do well to consider again the words of the fathers of Vatican Council II:

> The purpose, therefore, which priests pursue by their ministry and life is the glory of God the Father as it is to be achieved in Christ. That glory consists in this: that men knowingly, freely, and gratefully accept what God has achieved perfectly through Christ, and manifest it in their whole lives.[134]

The time is ripe for priests to involve themselves with charismatic renewal. The renewal is becoming a powerful force for the renewal of the Church. The ministry of the priest to the Catholic charismatic renewal will be unto the glory of God the Father.

ABBREVIATIONS
IN NOTES AND BIBLIOGRAPHY

ASLU	—*As the Spirit Leads Us*, Ranaghan
BCC	—*Building Christian Communities*, Clark
"BSST:BA"	—*"Baptism in the Spirit and Speaking in Tongues: A Biblical Appraisal,"* Montague
CP	—*Catholic Pentecostals*, Ranaghan
CP: PE	—*Catholic Pentecostals: Problems in Evaluation*, McDonnell
CRS	—Charismatic Renewal Services
FE	—*Fire on Earth: What God Is Doing in the World Today*, R. Martin
GM	—*Gifts and Ministries*, Bittlinger
LH	—*The Laying On of Hands*, O'Connor
LSC	—*The Lord, the Spirit, and the Church*, Ranaghan
Malines Document	—*Theological and Pastoral Orientations on the Catholic Charismatic Renewal*
PMCC	—*The Pentecostal Movement in the Catholic Church*, O'Connor

PMW	—*Pentecost in the Modern World*, O'Connor
PR:CA	—*Parish Renewal: A Charismatic Approach*, G. Martin
RW	—*Riding the Wind*, Montague
WAWH	—*Where Are We Headed?*, Clark

Notes

1. George H. Williams and Edith Waldvogel, "A History of Speaking in Tongues and Related Gifts," *The Charismatic Movement*, Michael P. Hamilton, ed. (Eerdmans, Grand Rapids, Mich., 1975), pp. 66-70; T. Del Monte Sol, "Pentecostalism and the Doctrine of St. Teresa and St. John of the Cross," *Spiritual Life*, 17 (September 1971), pp. 21-33; Vinson Synan, "The Role of the Holy Spirit and Gifts of the Spirit in the Mystical Tradition," *One in Christ*, 10:2 (1974), pp. 193-202.

2. Louis Bouyer, "Charismatic Movements in History within the Church Tradition," *One in Christ*, 10:2 (1974), p. 148.

3. Williams and Waldvogel, p. 77.

4. Note how the Protestant churches, begun so often as a reaction against institutionalism, have themselves become institutionalized. Once again the balance theory holds true.

5. Larry Christenson, *A Message to the Charismatic Movement* (Dimension, Minneapolis, 1972), p. 15.

6. Walter J. Hollenweger, *The Pentecostals: The Charismatic Movement in the Churches* (Augsburg, Minneapolis, 1973), pp. 22-26. (One author, Edward O'Connor, in his *Pentecost in the Catholic Church*, p. 17, claims that the Topeka event occured on January 1, 1901. Another respected writer, Kevin Ranaghan, in his *Catholic Pentecostals*, p. 256, claims the same. Both works are cited below.)

7. Frederick Dale Bruner, *A Theology of the Holy Spirit: The Pentecostal Experience and the New Testament Witness* (Eerdmans, Grand Rapids, Mich., 1974), p. 23.

8. See table in Hollenweger, p. 25.

9. Hollenweger, pp. 291-295.

10. There are some contemporary Pentecostal leaders who recognize the irrationality and untenable nature of fundamentalism who are often shunned by Pentecostals but are definitely gaining in popularity. One notable is Donald Gee.

11. Hollenweger, p. 330.

12. Hollenweger, pp. 330-341; see also Don Basham, *Ministering the Baptism in the Holy Spirit* (Whitaker, Pa., 1971), entire volume.

13. Bruner, pp. 61-69.

14. Hollenweger, pp. 342-347, 353-373; Bruner, pp. 130-149; Donald Gee, *Concerning Spiritual Gifts* (Gospel, Missouri, 1972), entire volume, and *Spiritual Gifts in the Work of the Ministry Today* (Gospel, Missouri, 1963), entire volume; Howard M. Ervin, *And Forbid Not to Speak with Tongues* (Logos, N.J., 1971), entire volume; and John L. Sherrill, *They Speak with Other Tongues* (Spire-Revell, N.J., 1968), entire volume.

15. Bruner, pp. 132-138.

16. Hollenweger, pp. 399-410.

17. Hollenweger, pp. 413-421.

18. Hollenweger, pp. 424-451.

19. Hollenweger, pp. 337-383; Don Basham, *Deliver Us from Evil* (Chosen, Connecticut, 1972), entire volume; Hobart E. Freeman, *Angels of Light?* (Logos, N.J., 1971), entire volume; and Raphael Gasson, *The Challenging Counterfeit* (Logos, N.J., 1972), entire volume.

20. Hollenweger, pp. 385-396.

21. Some would include the Pentecostal development in the Catholic Church under the title of Neo-Pentecostal. This is not accurate. We shall discuss the Catholics separately quite purposefully. The distinction is principally doctrinal.

22. Bruner, pp. 52-54.

23. Kilian McDonnell, *Catholic Pentecostalism: Problems in Evaluation* (Dove, New Mexico, 1970), p. 14.

24. Kevin and Dorothy Ranaghan, *Catholic Pentecostals* (Paulist, N.Y., 1969), p. 22. (For the personal testimonies of four persons on this weekend, see pp. 24-37.)

25. Ranaghan, *CP*, pp. 22-23.

26. Ranaghan, *CP*, pp. 38-57; Edward D. O'Con-

nor, *The Pentecostal Movement in the Catholic Church* (Ave Maria, Indiana, 1973), pp. 39-60.

27. O'Connor, *PMCC*, p. 35.

28. For fuller treatment of 1967-1970, see O'Connor, *PMCC*, pp. 15-18, 85-107; and James Connolly, C.S.C., "The Charismatic Movement: 1967-1970," *As the Spirit Leads Us*, Kevin and Dorothy Ranaghan, eds. (Paulist Press, New York, 1971), pp. 211-232.

29. O'Connor, *PMCC*, p. 35.

30. George Martin, *An Introduction to the Catholic Charismatic Renewal* (Word of Life, Ann Arbor, Mich., 1975), p. 2.

31. Edward D. O'Connor, *Pentecost in the Catholic Church* (Dove, New Mexico, 1970), p. 18.

32. Balthasar Fischer, "The Meaning of the Expression 'Baptism of the Spirit' in the Light of Catholic Baptismal Liturgy and Spirituality," *One in Christ*, 10:2 (1974), pp. 172-173; *Theological and Pastoral Orientations on the Catholic Charismatic Renewal* (prepared at Malines, Belgium, May 21-26, 1974) (Word of Life, N.D., Indiana, 1974), pp. 29-30, hereafter cited as *Malines Document*.

33. James D. G. Dunn, *Baptism in the Holy Spirit, Studies in Biblical Theology* (second series—15, SCM Press Ltd., London, 1974). For a shorter treatment, see Canon J. Giblet, "Baptism in the Spirit in Acts of the Apostles," *One in Christ*, 10:2 (1974), pp. 162-171.

34. For a sound criticism of Dunn, see George Montague, "Baptism in the Spirit and Speaking in Tongues: A Biblical Appraisal," *Theo Dig*, 21 (Winter 1973), pp. 242-260.

35. Donatien Mollat, "The Role of Experience in the New Testament Teaching on Baptism and the Coming of the Holy Spirit," *One in Christ*, 10:2 (1974), p. 129.

36. Mollat, p. 139.

37. Mollat, p. 147.

38. Edward Schillebeeckx, *Christ the Sacrament of the Encounter with God* (Sheed and Ward, N.Y., 1963), p. 182.

39. J. McHale, "The Charismatic Renewal Movement," *Furrow*, 24 (May 1973), pp. 259-271.

40. For more explanation of the experience of faith,

see Leon Cardinal Suenens, *A New Pentecost?* (Crossroad Book, Seabury Press, N.Y., 1975), pp. 50-70.

41. O'Connor, *PMCC*, p. 136.

42. George Martin, *An Introduction. . . .*, p. 5.

43. Simon Tugwell, *Did You Receive the Spirit?* (Paulist, N.Y., 1971), p. 43; P. Hocken, "Catholic Pentecostalism: Some Key Questions-I," *Heythrop*, 15 (April 1974), pp. 131-143.

44. Francis A. Sullivan, S.J., " 'Baptism in the Holy Spirit': A Catholic Interpretation of the Pentecostal Experience," *Gregorianum*, 55:1 (1974), esp. pp. 61-66.

45. James Byrne, *Threshold of God's Promise* (Ave Maria, Indiana, 1972), pp. 48-49.

46. Edward D. O'Connor, *The Laying on of Hands* (Dove, New Mexico, 1969).

47. Suenens, p. 82.

48. Stephen B. Clark, *Spiritual Gifts* (Dove, New Mexico, 1969), pp. 9-23.

49. Arnold Bittlinger, *Gifts and Ministries* (Eerdmans, Grand Rapids, Mich., 1973), p. 15.

50. *Summa* Ia-IIae, question 111, a. 1, ad 3.

51. Bittlinger, *GM*, p. 18.

52. See note 50.

53. Malines Document, pp. 50-51.

54. Montague, "BSST:BA," pp. 350-360.

55. George T. Montague, *Riding the Wind* (Word of Life, Ann Arbor, Mich., 1974), pp. 17-18.

56. Suenens, p. 100.

57. William J. Samarin, *Tongues of Men and Angels* (N.Y., 1972).

58. Malines Document, p. 52.

59. Peter Hocken, "Catholic Pentecostalism: Some Key Questions-II," *Heythrop*, 15 (July 1974), pp. 271-284.

60. See also Arnold Bittlinger, *Gifts and Graces* (Eerdmans, Grand Rapids, Mich., 1972), pp. 99-106; Montague, *RW*, pp. 44-48; O'Connor, *PMCC*, pp. 121-131; Suenens, pp. 99-104; Tugwell, pp. 66-74; and Rev. Vincent M. Walsh, *A Key to Charismatic Renewal in the Catholic Church* (Abbey Press, St. Meinrad, Ind., 1975), pp. 48-63.

61. Malines Document, pp. 54-55.

62. Cf. bibliography for numerous reference materials.

63. Malines Document, p. 7.

64. Malines Document, p. 10.

65. Kevin Ranaghan, *The Lord, the Spirit, and the Church* (CRS, Notre Dame, 1973), p. 34.

66. Canon J. Giblet, "Baptism in the Acts of the Apostles," *One in Christ*, 10:2 (1974), p. 165.

67. Suenens, p. 95.

68. Suenens, pp. 56-57.

69. Giblet, pp. 126-128.

70. Stephen B. Clark, "Charismatic Renewal in the Church," *As the Spirit Leads Us*, Kevin and Dorothy Ranaghan, eds. (Paulist Press, N.Y., 1971), p. 22.

71. Edward D. O'Connor, *Pentecost in the Modern World* (Ave Maria, Indiana, 1972), pp. 22-40; see also A. Fedders, "The Holy Spirit in the Church Today: The Charismatic Movement," *Priest*, 31 (June 1975), pp. 15-23; and Bro. J. O'Neill, "Charismatic Renewal and Its Spirituality," *Furrow*, 25 (November 1974), pp. 599-603.

72. O'Connor, *PMCC*, p. 116.

73. James Cavnar, "Dynamics of the Prayer Meeting," in *ASLU* by Ranaghan, pp. 60-65.

74. Stephen Clark, *Where Are We Headed?* (CRS, Notre Dame, 1973), p. 33.

75. O'Connor, *PMCC*, pp. 112-120.

76. Byrne, p. 58.

77. Hocken, II, p. 271; O'Connor, *LH*, entire work; Malines Document, pp. 57-58.

78. O'Connor, *PMCC*, p. 115; James Cavnar, *Prayer Meetings* (Dove, New Mexico, 1969), pp. 14-16; and for a broader exposition of prayer meetings see Jim Cavnar, *Participating in Prayer Meetings* (Word of Life, Ann Arbor, Mich., 1974), entire volume.

79. Ralph Martin, *Fire on Earth: What God Is Doing in the World Today* (Word of Life, Ann Arbor, Mich., 1975), p. 34.

80. Ranaghan, *LSC*, p. 53.

81. Ranaghan, *LSC*, p. 28.

82. O'Connor, *PMW*, p. 42.

83. Bert Ghezzi, "The End of the Catholic Pentecos-

tal Movement," *Sign*, 51 (November 1971), p. 10.

84. Clark, *WAWH*, pp. 9, 14, 17, 31, 34, 38.

85. Ralph Martin, *FE*, p. 72.

86. Report of the Committee on Doctrine of the NCCB submitted to the bishops on November 14, 1969 at Washington, D.C., reprinted in *PMCC* by Edward O'Connor, pp. 291-293, and in *CP:PE* by Kilian McDonnell, pp. 43-46.

87. Joseph McKinney, "The Bishops, Atlanta, 1972," *New Cov*, 1:12 (June 1972), p. 10.

88. *Lumen Gentium*, n. 12; see also "Charismatic Renewal: A Message of the Canadian Bishops," *Cath Mind*, 74 (October 1975), pp. 55-64.

89. Entire text reproduced in *New Cov*, 15:1 (July 1975), pp. 23-25.

90. Archbishop James Hayes, "Renewal of the Church," *New Cov*, 4:3 (September 1974), pp. 12-13.

91. R. Eimer, "The Catholic Pentecostal Movement," *Priest*, 27 (March 1971), pp. 35-43; O'Connor, *PMCC*, pp. 221-233; Malines Document, pp. 37-42; Kilian McDonnell, O.S.B., "Ecumenical Notes and Documentation," *One in Christ*, 10:2 (1974), pp. 213-214.

92. Donald L. Gelpi, *Pentecostal Piety* (Paulist, N.Y., 1972), pp. 61-72.

93. Clark, *WAWH*, pp. 23-26, 65-73.

94. All quotations in this chapter are from Walter M. Abbott, S.J., ed., *The Documents of Vatican II*, "Decree on the Ministry and Life of Priests" (Corpus Books, N.Y., 1966), pp. 532-576, unless otherwise noted.

95. From the *Rite of Ordination to the Diaconate*.

96. This and all subsequent references to "Decree" are presumed to be the "Decree on the Ministry and Life of Priests" as cited in note 94.

97. *Decree*, n. 13.

98. Cardinal Humberto Medeiros, "Priests: Guide Prayer Groups," *New Cov*, 3:10 (May 1974), p. 18.

99. Donald Gelpi, "Charismatic Renewal: Problems, Possibilities," *Nat Cath Rep*, 9 (August 3, 1973), p. 7.; see also Malines Document, p. 40.

100. Christensen, p. 101.

101. Ranaghan, *LSC*, pp. 51-52.

102. George Martin, *Parish Renewal: A Charismatic Approach,* "The Role of the Pastor" (Word of Life, Ann Arbor, Michigan, 1976), p. 79.

103. George Martin, *PR:CA,* p. 83.

104. Archbishop James Hayes, "Renewal of the Church," *New Cov,* 4:3 (September 1974), p. 12.

105. James E. Byrne, "Charismatic Leadership," in Ranaghan, *ASLU,* p. 191.

106. Many of the ideas above (after note 105) are borrowed from a presentation by Kevin Ranaghan entitled "The Relationship Between the Priest and the Layman," given in June 1975 at the first National Charismatic Conference for Priests in Steubenville, Ohio.

107. Edward O'Connor, from a presentation entitled "The Role of the Priest in Charismatic Renewal," given at Steubenville, 1975. See note 106.

108. Ranaghan, *LSC,* p. 51.

109. Walsh, p. 28.

110. Walsh, p. 263.

111. *Decree,* n. 9.

112. George Martin, *PR:CA,* pp. 86-87.

113. Walsh, p. 258.

114. Clark, BCC, p. 79.

115. Bittlinger, *GM,* p. 80.

116. O'Connor, *PMCC,* p. 223.

117. O'Connor, *PMCC,* p. 235.

118. See above, pp. 32-33, for references to this and the following dangers.

119. George Martin, *PR:CA,* p. 80.

120. Bishop Joseph McKinney, from a presentation entitled "Priests in Charismatic Renewal," delivered at Notre Dame, Indiana on June 16, 1974, at the International Conference for Charismatic Renewal.

121. Clark, *BCC,* p. 20.

122. Bro. David Steindl-Rast, "Charismatic Worship in the Catholic Church," *New Cov,* 4:7 (January 1975), p. 31.

123. Gelpi, "CR:PP," p. 7.

124. Clark, *BCC,* pp. 170-171.

125. O'Connor, *PMCC,* p. 236.

126. O'Connor, *PMCC,* pp. 237-238.

127. Walsh, p. 262.

128. Walsh, p. 262.

129. George Martin, *PR:CA*, p. 84.

130. See above, pp. 29-32.

131. "Charismatic Renewal: A Message of the Canadian Bishops," *Cath Mind*, 74 (October 1975), pp. 55-64.

132. Walsh, p. 260.

133. George Martin, *PR:CA*, pp. 85-86, 91.

134. *Decree*, n. 2.

Bibliography

BOOKS

Abbot, Walter M., S.J., ed. *The Documents of Vatican II*, Corpus Books, New York, 1966, 792 pp.

Agrimson, J. Elmo, ed. *Gifts of the Spirit and the Body of Christ*, Augsburg, Minneapolis, 1974, 112 pp. Lutherans comment on scriptural, sociological, behavioral, and other aspects of the movement. Good bibliographies.

Basham, Don. *Deliver Us From Evil*, Chosen, Connecticut, 1972, 222 pp. The witness of a well-known Protestant minister of deliverance.

————. *Face Up with a Miracle,* Voice, California, 1969, 191 pp. A personal witness by a Disciples of Christ minister to life in the Spirit.

————. *A Handbook on Tongues, Interpretation, and Prophecy*, Whitaker, Pa., 1971, 123 pp. Some good points; hazy scriptural derivations.

————. *Ministering the Baptism in the Holy Spirit,* Whitaker, Pa., 1971, 64 pp. Some good advice to ministers, demands cautious reading.

Bittlinger, Arnold. *Gifts and Graces*, Eerdmans, Grand Rapids, Mich., 1972, 126 pp. A scholarly commentary on 1 Corinthians 12—14.

————. *Gifts and Ministries,* Eerdmans, Grand Rapids, Mich., 1973, 109 pp. Discussion of the New Testament ministries as charisms, insights for today.

Bixler, Russell. *It Can Happen to Anybody*, Whitaker, Pa., 1970, 121 pp. A well-written personal testimony by a man called to the ministry.

Bruner, Frederick Dale. *A Theology of the Holy Spirit, the Pentecostal Experience and the New Testament Witness*, Eerdmans, Grand Rapids, Mich., 1974,

390 pp. A New Testament analysis of the experience and theology of the Holy Spirit. A challenge to classical Pentecostal doctrine.

Byrne, James. *Threshold of God's Promise*, Ave Maria, Indiana, 1972, 78 pp. A preparation for being baptized in the Spirit; comments, testimonies, and practical guides.

Carothers, Merlin R. *Power in Praise*, Logos, N.J., 1972, 115 pp. The value and usefulness of praising God—an extreme position.

Cavnar, Jim. *Participating in Prayer Meetings*, Word of Life, Ann Arbor, Mich., 1974. Discussion of the dynamics of prayer meetings.

———. *Prayer Meetings*, Dove, New Mexico, 1969, 35 pp. An early proposal of what charismatic renewal prayer meetings are all about.

Christenson, Larry. *A Message to the Charismatic Movement*, Dimension, Minneapolis, 1972, 119 pp. The Catholic Apostolic Church is a notable forerunner of the charismatic renewal of today, from the 1830's in England. Speaks to the Church today.

Clark, Stephen B. *Building Christian Communities*, Ave Maria, Indiana, 1972, 189 pp. A clear thinker brings sound examination to the needs of the Church today—particular value for pastors.

———. *Confirmation and the Baptism of the Holy Spirit*, Dove, New Mexico, 1969, 20 pp. Brief discussion of baptism in the Holy Spirit as an experience of the effects of confirmation.

———. Growing in Faith, CRS, Notre Dame, 1972, 63 pp. An inspired commentary on living faith.

———. *Knowing God's Will*, Word of Life, Ann Arbor, 1974, 66 pp. Some good advice about discerning God's plans for our lives.

———. *Spiritual Gifts*, Dove, New Mexico, 1969, 33 pp. Brief statement on the nature and purpose of the gifts.

———. *Where Are We Headed?* CRS, Notre Dame, 1973, 80 pp. An excellent prognosis; proposes the proper direction for the charismatic renewal.

Coleman, Robert E. *The Master Plan of Evangelism*, Revell, N.J., 1970, 126 pp. A structure for evangelizing based on Jesus' "method."

Dunn, James D. G. *Baptism in the Holy Spirit*, Studies in Biblical Theology, Second Series-15, SCM Press Ltd., London, 1974, 248 pp. An excellent exegetical critique of the classical Pentecostal doctrine of baptism in the Holy Spirit, and a perhaps unwitting defense of the Catholic position.

Ervin, Howard M. *And Forbid Not To Speak with Tongues*, Logos, N.J., 1971, 78 pp. A Baptist pastor defends tongues.

Freeman, Hobart E. *Angels of Light?* Logos, N.J., 1971, 85 pp. A Southern Baptist speaks on demons, attributing many evils to them.

Frost, Robert C. *Overflowing Life*, Logos, N.J., 1971, 140 pp. Devotional life and personal ministry discussed in a charismatic framework.

————. *Set My Spirit Free,* Logos, N.J., 1973, 234 pp. Descriptive and experiential reflections on the Holy Spirit in Scripture.

Gasson, Raphael. *The Challenging Counterfeit*, Logos, N.J., 1972, 159 pp. A former spiritualist describes spiritualism and tells how it draws one away from the Christian life.

Gee, Donald. *Concerning Spiritual Gifts*, Gospel, Missouri, 1972, 119 pp. Discussion on particular charismatic gifts—somewhat hasty.

————. *Fruitful or Barren,* Gospel, Missouri, 1961, 89 pp. A Protestant charismatic interprets the nine fruits of the Holy Spirit from Galatians 5:22.

————. *Now That You've Been Baptized in the Spirit,* Gospel, Missouri, 1972, 175 pp. Toward greater maturity in Christian living, and a look at the New Testament ministries.

————. *Spiritual Gifts in the Work of the Ministry Today*, Gospel, Missouri, 1963, 101 pp. A discussion of ministerial gifts; weak.

Gelpi, Donald L. *Pentecostalism, A Theological Viewpoint*, Paulist, N.Y., 1971, 234 pp. An organized, systematic approach.

————. *Pentecostal Piety,* Paulist, N.Y., 1972, 97 pp.

Healing as a regular Church ministry; thoughts on ecumenism and conversion.

Geraets, David. *Baptism of Suffering*, Dove, New Mexico, 1970, 43 pp. Notes on the positive side of suffering (physical and spiritual).

Hamilton, Michael P., ed. *The Charismatic Movement*, William B. Eerdmans, Grand Rapids, Mich., 1975, 196 pp. A diverse collection of articles concerning the background and development of charismatic renewal.

Hinnebusch, Paul. *Friendship in the Lord*, Ave Maria, Indiana, 1974, 144 pp. A beautiful document on friendship as an extension of the love of God.

Hollenweger, Walter J. *The Pentecostals: The Charismatic Movement in the Churches*, Augsburg, Minneapolis, Minn., 1973, 572 pp. Part I: A world history of the Pentecostals, much detail, little synthesis. Part II: Description of the doctrinal and experiential dimensions of many Pentecostal sects.

Kosicki, George, ed. *The Lord Is My Shepherd*, CRS, Ann Arbor, Mich., 1973, 129 pp. Thirteen priests describe their personal benefit from being involved in the charismatic renewal.

MacDonald, William G. *Glossolalia in the New Testament*, Gospel, Missouri, 1964, 20 pp. Technical, not careful.

MacNutt, Francis. *Healing*, Ave Maria, Indiana, 1974, 333 pp. Reflections on and witness of healing; practical and thoughtful, slightly redundant, excellent content.

Martin, George. *Introduction to the Catholic Charismatic Renewal*, Word of Life, Ann Arbor, Mich., 1975, 15 pp. A fine introductory pamphlet.

_____. *Parish Renewal: A Charismatic Approach*.

Martin, Ralph. *Hungry for God*, Doubleday, N.Y., 1974, 168 pp. A spiritual handbook for the modern Christian—excellent, charismatic.

_____. *Unless the Lord Build the House*, Ave Maria, Indiana, 1971, 62 pp. A biting statement urging the renewal of the Church to be not formless but based on Christ.

———. *Fire on the Earth: What God Is Doing in the World Today*, Word of Life, Ann Arbor, Mich., 1975, 94 pp. A good look at the world of today, charismatic renewal as the hope for the world.

McDonnell, Kilian. *Catholic Pentecostalism: Problems in Evaluation*, Dove, New Mexico, 1970, 58 pp. Bibliographies, astute observations, favorable evaluation.

———, and Arnold Bittlinger. *The Baptism in the Holy Spirit as an Ecumenical Problem*, CRS, Notre Dame, Indiana, 1972, 53 pp. A statement on Christian initiation and a comment on baptism in the Holy Spirit.

———, ed. *The Holy Spirit and Power: The Catholic Charismatic Renewal*, Doubleday, N.Y., 1975, 186 pp.

Montague, George T. *Riding the Wind*, Word of Life, Ann Arbor, Mich., 1974, 98 pp. A Scripture scholar speaks of his spirituality, of tongues, etc.

Mumford, Bob. *Take Another Look at Guidance*, Logos, N.J., 1971, 156 pp. Valuable insights into living according to God's will.

Mussner, Franz. *What Did Jesus Teach About the End of the World?* Word of Life, Ann Arbor, Mich., 1974, 69 pp. Too literal in an approach to Mark's Gospel, not sensitive to Mark's role in the textual composition.

Nee, Watchman. *The Release of the Spirit*, Sure Foundation, Cloverdale, Indiana, 1965, 94 pp. A thought-provoking volume on brokenness as a requisite for the work of the Holy Spirit.

O'Connor, Edward D. *The Laying on of Hands*, Dove, New Mexico, 1969, 21 pp. Biblical and contemporary significance.

———. *The Pentecostal Movement in the Catholic Church*, Ave Maria, Indiana, 1973, 301 pp. A classic work, broad and accurate; historical elements, theological reflections, bibliography.

———. *Pentecost in the Catholic Church*, Dove, New Mexico, 1970, 38 pp. A brief introduction to charismatic renewal; answers pertinent questions.

_____. *Pentecost in the Modern World,* Ave Maria, In-
diana, 1972, 48 pp. Brief discussion of the role of
charismatic renewal in the Church and the world.

_____, ed. *Perspectives on Charismatic Renewal,* U. of
Notre Dame, Indiana, 1975, 216 pp. Background
essays on charismatic renewal, plus an extended,
annotated bibliography.

Prince, Derek. *How To Judge Prophecy,* Prince, Florida,
1971, 19 pp. Nine considerations in testing the genuineness of prophecy.

_____. *Restoration Through Fasting,* Prince, Florida,
1970, 27 pp. A scriptural commentary on fasting.

Ranaghan, Kevin. *The Lord, the Spirit and the Church,*
CRS, Notre Dame, Indiana, 1973, 61 pp. Statements on the purpose and goals of charismatic renewal.

_____, and Dorothy, eds. *As the Spirit Leads Us,* Paulist,
N.Y., 1971, 250 pp. A series of essays on charismatic renewal's nature, goals, value, history, direction,
and purpose; most are good.

_____, and Dorothy. *Catholic Pentecostals,* Paulist,
N.Y., 1969, 266 pp. The origins of and early reflections on charismatic renewal; still good.

Randall, John. *In God's Providence: The Birth of a Catholic Charismatic Parish,* Living Flame, N.Y., 1973,
66 pp. A living account.

Samarin, William J. *Tongues of Men and Angels,* N.Y.,
1972. An anthropological and linguistic study of
praying in tongues.

Scanlan, Michael. *Inner Healing,* Paulist, N.Y., 1974, 85
pp. The theory and practice of healing not limbs
but the intellectual, volitional, and affective parts of
man. Important.

_____. *The Power in Penance,* Ave Maria, Indiana, 1972.
An insightful and valuable statement on the sacrament of penance.

Schillebeeckx, Edward. *Christ the Sacrament of the Encounter with God,* Sheed and Ward, N.Y., 1963,
222 pp. A solid, thought-provoking treatment of
sacramental theology.

Sherrill, John L. *They Speak with Other Tongues,* Spire
(Revel), N.J., 1968, 143 pp. A reporter's skeptical,

then committed involvement with Pentecostals.

Statement on Catholic Charismatic Renewal, Committee for Pastoral Research and Practice, NCCB, Washington, D.C., 1975, 9 pp.

Suenens, Leon Joseph Cardinal. *A New Pentecost?* Crossroad Book, Seabury Press, N.Y., 1975. A man of wisdom reflects on his Church and the charismatic experience. Excellent, substantive.

Theological and Pastoral Orientations on the Catholic Charismatic Renewal (prepared at Malines Belgium, May 21-26, 1974), Word of Life, Indiana, 1974, 71 pp. An important statement by competent theologians.

Tugwell, Simon. *Did You Receive the Spirit?* Paulist, N.Y., 1971, 143 pp. Important theological statement, objective evaluation of charismatic renewal, favorable.

Walsh, Rev. Vincent M. *A Key to Charismatic Renewal in the Catholic Church*, Abbey Press, St. Meinrad, Indiana, 1975, 286 pp. Good perspective on charismatic renewal, excellent explanations of the charisms and prayer groups, sometimes inaccurate with Scripture. Author: Philadelphia's Vice-Chancellor.

PERIODICALS

Amalfitano, Frank. "Identity Crisis," *New Cov*, 1:12 (June 1972), pp. 18-19. A strong statement about why priests today have identity problems: they're not free to minister as they know they must.

Baum, Gregory. "On the Charismatic Renewal," *New Cov*, 1:12 (June 1972), pp. 12-13, 23 (reprinted from the *St. Louis Review*). An enthusiastic plug for the value for Pentecostals of taking on some of the traditions the Catholic Church has to offer.

Baum, Archbishop William. "The Search for Unity: The Charismatic Renewal and Ecumenism," *New Cov*, 5:7 (January 1976), pp. 22-24. An exploration of some ecumenical possibilities as influenced by charismatic renewal.

Bouyer, Louis. "Charismatic Movements in History within the Church Tradition," *One in Christ*, 10:2

(1974), pp. 148-161. Such movements are ever reoc-
curring in the Church.

Brennan, J. "Ministry of Healing," *Priest*, 31 (May 1975),
pp. 14-16, 19, and (June 1975), pp. 33-41. Healings
are occurring; explanation of what they are all
about and how to pray for healing. Well done.

Cavnar, Jim. "Spiritual Gifts in the Prayer Meeting,"
New Cov, 5:5 (November 1975), pp. 12-15. The
Spirit works powerfully through the gifts in the
context of the prayer meeting.

"Charismatic Renewal: A Message of the Canadian Bishops," *Cath Mind*, 74 (October 1975), pp. 55-64.
The bishops state their opinion regarding the renewal. Overall favorable observations.

Cornwell, D. "Amazing Grace Gift," *America*, 130 (July
27, 1974), p. 32. A doctor's witness to his own son's
healing.

Dearden, Cardinal John. "A Living Church," *New Cov*,
4:5 (November 1974), pp. 24-25. A Pentecost homi-
ly to Detroit's prayer groups at Blessed Sacrament
Cathedral.

Del Monte Sol, T. "Pentecostalism and the Doctrine of
Saint Teresa and St. John of the Cross," *Spir Life*,
17 (September 1971), pp. 21-33. A Carmelite nun
relates elements of Pentecostalism to Teresa's and
John's spirituality, finding many similarities, especially with the former.

DuPlessis, David J. "The Historic Background of Pentecostalism," *One in Christ*, 10:2 (1974), pp. 174-
179. Pentecostalism's roots in the first century.

Eimer, R. "The Catholic Pentecostal Movement," *Priest*,
27 (March 1971), pp. 35-43. A priest lists some objective positive and negative criticisms.

Ellis, E. Earle. "Spiritual Gifts in the Pauline Community," *NTS*, 20:2 (January 1974), pp. 128-144. An
analysis of Paul's conceptions of *pneumatika* as not
only Paul's theory, but Paul's experience.

Fedders, A. "The Holy Spirit in the Church Today: The
Charismatic Movement," *Priest*, 31 (June 1975),
pp. 15-23. Charismatic renewal is of benefit for the
Church today, especially in ecumenical, missionary,
and ministerial activities.

Fichter, Joseph H. "How It Looks to a Social Scientist," *New Cath World*, 217 (November-December 1974), pp. 244-248. Unexpected social behavioral patterns seem to occur more than predictable patterns.

Fischer, Balthasar. "The Meaning of the Expression 'Baptism of the Spirit' in the Light of Catholic Baptismal Liturgy and Spirituality," *One in Christ*, 10:2 (1974), pp. 172-173. The terminological difficulty.

Futrell, J. "Charismatic Renewal in Historical Perspective," *Rev Rel*, 34 (January 1975), pp. 78-87. Charismatic renewal is good and appropriate in today's world. It needs theological and pastoral guidance. It must recognize other forms of spirituality.

Gelpi, Donald L. "Can You Institutionalize the Spirit?" *New Cath World*, 217 (November-December 1974), pp. 254-258. The relationship of Church to charisms.

———. "Charismatic Renewal: Problems, Possibilities," *Nat Cath Rep*, 9 (August 3, 1973), pp. 7+. The need and desire for clergy involvement is great; reasons for its absence.

Ghezzi, B. "The End of the Catholic Pentecostal Movement," *Sign*, 51 (November 1971), pp. 10-12+. The movement will end when the Church is renewed. Mentions some of the elements of our tradition being renewed in the movement.

Giblet, Canon J. "Baptism in the Spirit in the Acts of the Apostles," *One in Christ*, 10:2 (1974), pp. 162-171. Conversion, baptism, and reception of the Holy Spirit as the three elements of Christian initiation's single act.

Haglof, A. "Psychology and the Pentecostal Experience," *Spir Life*, 17 (Fall 1971), pp. 198-210. Analytic psychology gives its opinions on conversion and baptism in the Holy Spirit.

Harrington, D. "Baptism in the Holy Spirit: A Review Article," *Chic Stud*, 11 (September 1972), pp. 31-44. A comparative review of F. D. Bruner's "A Theology of the Holy Spirit . . ." and J. D. G. Dunn's "Baptism in the Holy Spirit."

Haughey, J. "Healed and Healing Priests," *America*, 133 (August 2, 1975), pp. 46-48. A Jesuit theologian examines healings in the charismatic renewal of the Catholic priesthood; special reference to a Steubenville 1975 conference for priests.

Hayes, Archbishop James. "Renewal of the Church," *New Cov*, 4:3 (September 1974), pp. 12-13. A pastoral message from a Canadian bishop offers hope and encouragement.

Healey, John. "The Good News Is Power," *America*, 133 (August 2, 1975), pp. 49-50. A priest recalls the National Charismatic Conference for Priests at Steubenville, Ohio, 1975.

———. "Nigerian Odyssey: Encounters with the Spirit," *America*, 132 (April 5, 1975), pp. 256-258. Report on an October 1974 healing mission to Africa.

Hellwig, Monika K. "Our Tradition and the Spirit," *St. Anthony Mes*, 82:9 (February 1975), pp. 26-31. Present interest in the Spirit is simply a continuation of Christian teaching down through the centuries.

Hocken, Peter. "Catholic Pentecostalism: Some Key Questions-I," *Heythrop*, 15 (April 1974), pp. 131-143. Clear critical thinking; the distinction from classical Pentecostalism; discussion of baptism of the Spirit.

———. "Catholic Pentecostalism: Some Key Questions-II," *Heythrop*, 15 (July 1974), pp. 271-284. Discussion of laying on of hands, gifts of the Holy Spirit, glossolalia, the place of reason, and some conclusions.

———. "Pentecostals on Paper," *Clergy Rev,* 59 (November 1974), pp. 750-767. A survey of Pentecostal literature, large bibliography.

Kosicki, Fr. George. "A Broken Cedar," *New Cov*, 1:12 (June 1972), pp. 1-3, 32. A personal witness; some possibilities for priests' personal spiritual renewal.

MacNutt, Francis. "New Power for the Priesthood," *New Cov*, 5:4 (October 1975), pp. 7-9. Charismatic renewal has helped many priests experience new power in their lives and in their ministry.

Marc 'Hadour, Germain. "The Holy Spirit over the New World," *Clergy Rev*, 59 (March 1974), pp. 184-200, and (April 1974), pp. 246-269. Report and commentary on the Charismatic Conference at Notre Dame Indiana in 1973.

Martin, Ralph. "An Interview with Fr. Heribert Mühlen: Theologian of the Holy Spirit," *New Cov*, 4:1 (July 1974), pp. 3-6. Some thoughts and observations from a dogmatic theologian.

―――. "How Shall We Relate to Church?" *New Cath World*, 217 (November-December 1974), pp. 249-253. Historical development of the Church—charismatics' relationship to it.

McDonnell, Kilian. "Catholic Pentecostalism: Problems in Evaluation," *Theol Dig*, 19 (September 1971), pp. 46-51. Some objective observations. Good.

―――. "The Distinguishing Characteristics of the Charismatic-Pentecostal Spirituality," *One in Christ*, 10:2 (1974), pp. 117-128. Excellent. Clear and meaty.

―――. "The Ecumenial Significance of the Pentecostal Movement," *Worship*, 40 (December 1966), pp. 608-629. The movement as it crosses all Christian confessional boundaries. Often cited.

―――. "The Ideology of Pentecostal Conversion," *Jour Ecum Stud*, 5 (Winter 1968), pp. 105-126. Delineation of the ideals that explain the growth of Pentecostalism.

―――. "The International Roman Catholic-Pentecostal Dialogue: The Meeting of a Structural Church and a Movement," *One in Christ*, 10:1 (1974), pp. 4-6.

―――. "New Dimensions in Research on Pentecostalism," *Worship* 45 (April 1971), pp. 214-219. Bibliography.

―――. "Statement of the Theological Basis of the Cathlic Charismatic Renewal," *One in Christ*, 9:2 (1974), pp. 206-215. Good.

McGrath, Frank. "God Saving His People," *New Cov*, 1:12 (June 1972), pp. 14-17. Personal witness plus thoughts on what effects the charismatic renewal has on priesthood.

McHale, J. "The Charismatic Renewal Movement," *Furrow*, 24 (May 1973), pp. 259-271. Charismatic renewal as the personal appropriation of what is already given in the Church.

McKinney, Bishop Joseph. "The Bishops, Atlanta, 1972,"

New Cov, 1:12 (June 1972), pp. 10-11. A report on the bishops' discussion of charismatic renewal, and a report given by Bishop John Quinn to the NCCB on April 13, 1972.

―――. "An Open Letter to Priests," *New Cov*, 1:12 (June 1972), pp. 8-9. Jesus Christ is Lord―the theme of our Church.

McTernan, John. "Water Baptism," *One in Christ*, 10:2 (1974), pp. 203-205. Argument for the separation of water baptism and the reception of the Holy Spirit (classical stance).

Medeiros, Cardinal Humberto. "Priests: Guide Prayer Groups," *New Cov*, 3:10 (May 1974), p. 18 (reprinted from the *Boston Pilot*, a 1974 pastoral letter to priests). Encourages priests to become available to prayer groups to guide their growth and avoid abuses.

Mollat, Donatien. "The Role of Experience in the New Testament Teaching on Baptism and the Coming of the Holy Spirit," *One in Christ*, 10:2 (1974), pp. 129-147. Experience as a common element of New Testament spirituality.

Montague, G. "Baptism in the Spirit and Speaking in Tongues: A Biblical Appraisal," *Theo Dig*, 21 (Winter 1973), pp. 342-360, an address before CBA on August 1, 1973. An amazingly competent study, scholarly and unbiased. Good bibliography.

Hauer, B. "The Intellectual and the Charismatics," *America*, 130 (July 27, 1974), pp. 26-29. Discussion of the intellectual's problems with charismatic renewal, and some solutions.

Nouwen, H. "The Pentecostal Movement: Three Perspectives," *Scholastic*, 109 (April 21, 1967), pp. 15-17, 32.

―――. "*A Catholic Pentecostal Movement* by E. O'Connor. A Critical Analysis by H. Nouwen," (Symposium) *Ave*, 105 (June 1967), pp. 6-13+. O'Connor's introduction to the movement. Nouwen's historical, psychological, and theological criticism. Objective, reveals some dangers, acknowledges positive aspects.

O'Connor, Edward D. "The Catholic Pentecostal Movement: A Theological Assessment," *Cath Theo Soc
of Am*, 24 (1969), pp. 90-108. Rejuvenation of be-
lief in and experience of the Holy Spirit.

O'Hanlon, D. "Pentecostals and Pope John's New Pentecost," *America*, 108 (May 1963), pp. 634-636. A
man of vision takes some lessons from the Pentecostal traditions, well before the Catholic renewal.

O'Meara, F. "Pentecostalism Is Not the Answer," *U.S.
Cath*, 38 (December 1973), pp. 14-16. Sharp criticism.

O'Neill, Bro. J. "Charismatic Renewal and Its Spirituality," *Furrow*, 25 (November 1974), pp. 599-603. A
spirituality answering a hunger for God. Prayer
groups are the most genuine forms of Christian
community in the parish setting. Rediscovering
praise.

Paul VI. "Pope Paul Addresses the Charismatic Renewal," *New Cov*, 5:1 (July 1975), pp. 23-25. The official text of the Pope's statement and a translation
of his informal remarks in Italian.

"The Pentecostal Movement in the Catholic Church in the
U.S.A., Report to the Semi-Annual Meeting of the
U.S. Catholic Bishops in Washington, D.C.," *Theo
Dig*, 19 (September 1971), pp. 52-53.

Rahner, Karl. "Meditation on the Renewal of Priestly Ordination," *New Cov*, 1:12 (June 1972), pp. 12-13,
reprinted from *Theological Investigations*, Vol. III.
Comments on renewal of ordination, an event
which is seen today in the Catholic charismatic renewal.

Ranaghan, Kevin. "Catholic Charismatic Renewal: The
First Seven Years," *New Cov*, 3:8 (March 1974),
pp. 3-6, adapted from his address to the 1st International Leaders Conference in Rome, October
1973. A spiritual state of the union; very good.

"The Roman Catholic-Pentecostal Dialogue; Symposium," *One in Christ*, 10:2 (1974), pp. 106-205.

Scanlan, Michael. "Meeting Jesus in the Sacraments,"
New Cov, 5:4 (October 1975), pp. 17-19. A priest in

charismatic renewal calls for renewal of the sacramental experience of God.

Steindl-Rast, Bro. David. "Charismatic Worship in the Catholic Church," *New Cov*, 4:7 (January 1975), pp. 30-31. Charismatic renewal is renewing the worship of the Church; implications for bishops and priests.

Suenens, Cardinal Leon Josef. "The Pentecostal Movement: An Interview," *Tablet*, 227 (August 18, 1973), pp. 789-791. An enthusiastic evaluation of charismatic renewal from the heart of the Church.

Sullivan, Francis A., S.J. "Baptism in the Holy Spirit: A Catholic Interpretation of the Pentecostal Experience," *Gregorianum*, 55 (1974), pp. 49-68. Interpretation of baptism in the Holy Spirit in the light of Thomas' *On the Sending of the Divine Persons*.

Synan, Vinson. "The Role of the Holy Spirit and the Gifts of the Spirit in the Mystical Tradition," *One in Christ*, 10:2 (1974), pp. 193-202. Suggests a close parallel between Pentecostals and mystics.

Wild, Robert. "Bultmann and the Charismatic Renewal," *Cross and Crown*, 26 (June 1974), pp. 174-185. How the charismatic renewal can contribute to the demythologization of Scripture. The charismatic renewal is a providential conditioning factor for scriptural interpretation today.

———. "The Spirit in the New Testament," *St. Anthony Mes*, 82 (February 1975), pp. 14-19. Today's renewal of the Spirit is parallel to the experience of and guidance by him in Acts.

Williams, Dr. Rodman. "Pentecostal Spirituality," *One in Christ*, 10:2 (1974), pp. 180-192. Focuses on baptism of the Spirit.

Wright, John H. "Discernment of Spirits in the New Testament," *Communio*, 1 (Summer 1974), pp. 115-127. Examination of some New Testament data on discerning spirits and seeking God's will.

Yocum, Bruce. "Growing in the Use of Spiritual Gifts," *New Cov*, 5:5 (November 1975), pp. 9-11. How a person cooperates with the Lord in order for his spiritual gifts to mature.